FROM STATEHOUSE
TO COURTHOUSE

HISTORIC CHARLESTON FOUNDATION
STUDIES IN HISTORY AND CULTURE

Historic Preservation for a Living City:
Historic Charleston Foundation, 1947–1997
Robert R. Weyeneth

From Statehouse to Courthouse:
An Architectural History of South Carolina's Colonial
Capitol and Charleston County Courthouse
Carl R. Lounsbury

FROM STATEHOUSE
TO COURTHOUSE

An Architectural History of
South Carolina's Colonial Capitol
and Charleston County Courthouse

CARL R. LOUNSBURY

UNIVERSITY OF SOUTH CAROLINA PRESS

UNIVERSITY OF SOUTH CAROLINA *BICENTENNIAL*

© 2001 University of South Carolina

Published in Columbia, South Carolina, by the
University of South Carolina Press

Manufactured in the United States of America

05 04 03 02 01   5 4 3 2 1

Library of Congress Cataloging-in-Publication Data

Lounsbury, Carl.
   From statehouse to courthouse : an architectural history of South
Carolina's colonial capitol and Charleston County courthouse / Carl R.
Lounsbury.
       p. cm. — (Historic Charleston Foundation studies in history and culture)
   Includes bibliographical references (p.   ) and index.
   ISBN 1-57003-378-1 (cloth : alk. paper)
   1. Charleston County Courthouse (Charleston, S.C.) 2. Architecture—
Conservation and restoration—South Carolina—Charleston. 3. Architecture,
Colonial—South Carolina—Charleston. 4. Charleston (S.C.)—Buildings, struc-
tures, etc. I. Title. II. Series.
   NA4473.C48 L68   2001
   725'.15'09757915—dc21   00-010292

CONTENTS

FOREWORD

On 21 September 1989 Hurricane Hugo's 140-miles-per-hour winds tore through the Charleston County Courthouse at the northwest corner of Meeting and Broad Streets. A few months before the hurricane, Charleston solicitor Charles Condon had contacted staff members of Historic Charleston Foundation, as well as the Charleston County Bar Association and other concerned individuals, about the state of the courthouse and its surrounding buildings. In the wake of a proposal to study repair and renovation of the building, architects had already been hired by Charleston County to seek significant renovations. The aftermath of the hurricane made possible the rediscovery of the history of one of the most important buildings in Charleston and South Carolina. In the rejection of an initial offer from the Federal Emergency Management Authority for simple repairs to the structure, Charleston County administrator E. E. Fava stated that the building was so "historically significant we have a vested interest in not only the outside, but the inside."

The various interested parties came together before the hurricane to form the Friends of the Charleston County Courthouse. With the leadership of its initial chairman, Charlton DeSaussure, Jr., and later cochairs Mrs. Thomas Hartnett and attorney and historian Robert Rosen, this group attracted a coalition of local business people, preservationists, attorneys, and citizens to seek a significant understanding of the history of the courthouse and the proper measures for its rehabilitation.

With a grant from the National Trust for Historic Preservation, a symposium was convened by the Friends of the Charleston County Courthouse on 24 May 1990. Historians speaking at the event included the author of this work, Dr. Carl Lounsbury, architectural historian at Colonial Williamsburg, and William Seale, historian of the White House. Lounsbury, for a talk titled "The Charleston Court House as Provincial English Architecture," traced the background of the architecture and functions of courthouses in England and America and centered on his own preliminary research into the background of the Charleston building. Seale's lively presentation centered on his findings of the architectural relationship between the Charleston County Courthouse, the design of the White House, and the architectural work of James Hoban, Irish-born Charleston draftsman and architect of the White House. Other presenters included Dr. George Rogers, emeritus professor of history at the University of South Carolina; South Carolina Supreme Court Justice

viii   Jean Toal; Rosen; and the county's retained architect Dinos Liollio and consultant Neil Quenzel of John Milner Associates.

After tracing the history of the building in the context of South Carolina's governmental development in the late eighteenth century, Dr. Rogers told the symposium, "With so much history having swirled around the Charleston County Courthouse, we cannot fail to restore the building with the greatest care in the finest tradition of preservation." Justice Toal, in her remarks, thinking about the temporary move of the courts to a building near Rivers Avenue, added, "No matter whether you're in North Charleston, the courthouse is at the corner of Broad and Meeting." These remarks built upon a challenge from Linda Lombard, then chairman of Charleston County Council: "We bear a joint responsibility to ensure that the courthouse continues to contribute to the life of this community, both in terms of its physical presence and its function." She stated that the courthouse was "a magnificent structure" and "part of the heritage of this county, this state, indeed this nation."

Although Historic Charleston Foundation had already recognized the need for detailed historical study, calling on the county council as early as January 1991 to enter into an agreement for a Historic American Buildings Survey of the building and its fabric, efforts to convince the county to seek the detailed examination of the building, urged by Lounsbury and Dr. Bernard Herman at the University of Delaware, were, at this juncture, unsuccessful.

Nonetheless, as the county's own consultant began to urge that the building not be restored to its late-eighteenth-century appearance, the foundation retained Lounsbury and, later, W. Brown Morton III of Mary Washington College for a preliminary examination. Their cursory studies proved that the fabric of the Charleston County Courthouse could indeed be analyzed and provide further information on its original form. Also, they suggested that surviving records could be carefully gleaned for information to tell the story of the building and its significance. In June 1991 a team consisting of Morton and Lounsbury, with his colleagues Willie Graham and Mark Wenger of Colonial Williamsburg, came to Charleston for two weeks at the invitation of Historic Charleston Foundation. Armed with helpers as well as crowbars and sledgehammers, they removed selected later modern fabric to gather information, revealing brick walls, surviving framing, and other woodwork. At the end of the study the consultants were able to conclude that the building was definitely the original colonial statehouse, one of six surviving in the nation, and the only one in the South. This discovery, along with the historical documentation of the use of the building by the U.S. Supreme Court justices' riding circuit, as well as its occupation by the Charleston Library Society, the Medical Society of South Carolina, and the Charleston Museum, led Morton, author of the Secretary of Interior Standards, to call for the building's restoration. Morton stated that "this is a building of national, if not international significance. There is no building in South Carolina, with the possible exception of Fort Sumter, that is more historic—or that has been more abused."

Further information discovered by Lounsbury, with the assistance of staff members and interns of Historic Charleston Foundation, has yielded the background for a full architectural and social history of the Charleston statehouse and courthouse. More than five years of additional work by the county, its former and present architects, the foundation, and the Friends of the Courthouse (especially through the cochairmanship of Nancy Hawk and Rosen) have led to final agreements toward the building's restoration to its 1792 appearance despite several periods of delay due to cost concerns and other factors. The rear wing was removed in 1993, and extensive archaeology in the rear yard was completed. Now, as the county prepares farsightedly to construct a new, adjacent judicial center, additional archaeological investigation should prove illuminating.

Through renovations in 1883 and again in 1926, 1941, and 1968, more and more of the original historic fabric of the courthouse was obscured and lost, and more and more of the building's significance to the community was removed. A 1963 newspaper ad bore the headline "Courthouse in Need of Renovation," with the subtitle "Are the Taxpayers Willing to Pay for It?" The continued use of public funds in these transitory renovations not only harmed the building but also resulted in no final solution to securing a dignified courthouse for Charleston.

This volume is primarily an architectural history based on exceptional documentary and building research. It serves as a chronicle of the courthouse and a study in change over time and the detective work necessary to rescue such an important building from obscurity. The miraculous rediscovery of the early appearance and early history of this major public structure, as well as the ensuing debate over its restoration, exemplifies the ongoing story of historic preservation in Charleston, South Carolina. Through Lounsbury's splendid study it is the hope of the foundation and the Friends of the Charleston County Courthouse that the significance of the structure will finally be disseminated and that sufficient information will prevent it from ever languishing again in oblivion at the Civic Square.

There are many individuals and organizations that Historic Charleston Foundation, the writer of this foreword, and author Carl Lounsbury wish to thank for their roles in the analysis and study of the courthouse and to some degree the eventual restoration of the building. The commitment by the Foundation to the Courthouse and to this book has been attributable to the work of its Board of Trustees and Executive Committee members, especially its past presidents, Bachman S. Smith III, Thomas A. Palmer, John H. Warren III, J. Rutledge Young Jr., Harold R. Pratt-Thomas Jr., and Jane P. Hanahan. Historic Charleston Foundation staff and interns who labored on the work have included Carrie Albee, Rae Ann Blyth, Carroll Ann Bowers, Betty Guerard, Elizabeth Gukenberger, Amanda Griffith Herbert, Carter Hudgins, Dennis Hughes, Scott Lane, Therese Munroe, Louis Nelson, Danielle Palms, Katharine Robinson, Katherine Saunders, M. E. Van Dyke, Lawrence Walker, and Donna Williamson. Equally important, the courthouse has been rescued through the efforts of the Friends of the Charleston County Courthouse, especially Bonnie Hartnett,

x   Nancy Hawk, and Robert Rosen, along with cabinet members William Cathcart, Bart Daniel, Charlton deSaussure Jr., Hoyt Rowell, Brad Waring, former staff member Jane Stoney Cook, and development counsel June Bradham.

Various individuals assisted Carl Lounsbury and Historic Charleston Foundation in the documentation of the courthouse, especially W. Brown Morton of Mary Washington College, Mark R. Wenger and Willie Graham of Colonial Williamsburg Foundation, Richard Marks III, and architect Glenn Keyes. Additional help came from John Laurens, Ricardo Viera, Martha Zierden, and Joe Joseph of New South Associates, who conducted the archaeological investigation of the site. Steven Bauer was the preservationist (on site) for the first interior demolition phase of the courthouse project and spearheaded further documentation. Crucial documentation and research study also was provided by Robert Stockton, Wayne Jordan, Kinloch Bull, and the late Dr. George Rogers.

Thanks are also owed the staffs of the South Carolina Historical Society, the Gibbes Museum of Art, the Charleston Museum, the South Carolina Department of Archives and History, and the South Caroliniana Library of the University of South Carolina.

Historic Charleston Foundation extends its greatest appreciation for the commitment of successive members of the Charleston County Council, including chairman Barrett Lawrimore, and county staff, particularly retired county administrator E. E. Fava, as well as Guy Blanton, Roland Windham, and Jim Wigley. They have assured that the research conducted has been followed and the building has been returned, as much as possible, to its 1792 appearance.

Jonathan Poston
Historic Charleston Foundation

FROM STATEHOUSE
TO COURTHOUSE

INTRODUCTION

This study of the Charleston County Courthouse is intended to present a concise architectural history of one of South Carolina's most important but least understood buildings. The lack of awareness about the architectural significance of the courthouse derives, in no small part, from the rough treatment it has suffered since its initial construction in 1753. The disappearance of building records, a disastrous fire in 1788, two large additions, and at least four major renovations have obscured the intentions of the original design. Buried beneath subsequent accretions stand the remains of South Carolina's first and only colonial statehouse, perhaps the most ambitious civic structure erected in the American colonies in the eighteenth century. In the 1790s the building was substantially reconstructed as the county courthouse. Since then it has served as the central forum for interpreting the character of local

Charleston County Courthouse, 1883, photographed for Arthur Mazyck, *Charleston in 1883*. This view shows the courthouse as designed in 1792, before the alterations of 1883–1884 that eliminated the belt courses, lengthened the upper-story windows, extended the rustication around the entire ground floor, and changed the doorway on Meeting Street to appear as the principal entry.

2

Third-floor courtroom in the 1941 addition, damaged by Hurricane Hugo in 1989. Photograph by Willie Graham, Colonial Williamsburg Foundation, 1991.

justice, but few people today realize the broader role it once played in shaping the cultural life of the city in the late colonial and early national periods. At one time it housed one of America's earliest museums and served as the venue for discussions about the efficacy of various medical treatments by the city's physicians. Few visitors to Charleston in the early nineteenth century left without a visit to this stuccoed brick building on the northwest corner of Broad and Meeting Streets. It defined and symbolized the cultural accomplishments of the city.

Although the historical importance of the courthouse was acknowledged by Charlestonians in the early part of the twentieth century, few were inspired by the building.[1] With no local advocates, it rarely received wider recognition in surveys of early American architecture. In her study *The Architects of Charleston,* published in 1945, Beatrice St. Julien Ravenel noted that most observers agreed with the verdict passed on the building nearly a century earlier by the antebellum novelist and native Charlestonian William Gilmore Simms: "It is content to be big, solid, square, and lofty, serving its purposes, and making no fuss, and challenging no man's admiration."[2] The sentiments of Simms derived from an aesthetic far different from the one that inspired the original designers, but later alterations and the shabby appearance of the courthouse through much of the twentieth century invited little enthusiasm among preservationists. In constant need of a fresh coat of paint, the courthouse was a warren of corridors and tiny offices. As the legal system and standards of comfort changed over time, the courtrooms appeared hopelessly inadequate. Many judges and members of the bar who practiced there hardly recognized the building's antiquity

View of the Charleston County Courthouse from St. Michael's Church steeple, revealing damage by Hurricane Hugo in September 1989. Photograph by Jack Boucher, Historic American Buildings Survey, 1991.

or appreciated its architectural significance. A lawyer who began his career arguing cases in the principal courtroom thought it looked no better than a dingy bus station.[3]

When Hurricane Hugo wrecked the courthouse along with much of the city in September 1989, the architectural history of the building was still shrouded in a veil of mystery. It was uncertain whether anything of the colonial statehouse had survived the fire of 1788. Little was known about the plan and function of the building during its early days. Some documents provided fragmentary evidence of interior finishes, but no one could estimate the amount of early woodwork, plaster, and paint still existing beneath layers of modern drywall, contact wallpaper, and shag carpeting. The necessity of assessing the structural damage caused by Hugo provided the opportunity to carefully investigate the building's fabric in order that such questions might be answered.

A systematic study of the building revealed that much of the old statehouse remained intact, covered over by subsequent alterations. Even more material survived from the period of conversion of the statehouse to the county courthouse in the late eighteenth and early nineteenth centuries. Plaster, paint, floorboards, window jambs, studs, and roof framing provided tantalizing evidence of the furnishing and function of the early courts and government offices. However, a thorough renovation in 1883 destroyed much of the earlier woodwork. Most of what managed to escape this drastic gutting of the building gradually disappeared during subsequent alterations made to the building in the twentieth century. Fragments of earlier

4

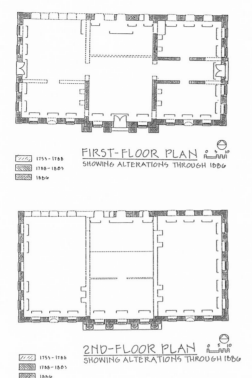

FIRST-FLOOR PLAN
SHOWING ALTERATIONS THROUGH 1886

2ND-FLOOR PLAN
SHOWING ALTERATIONS THROUGH 1886

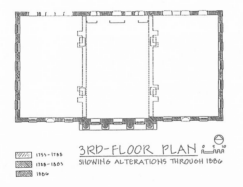

3RD-FLOOR PLAN
SHOWING ALTERATIONS THROUGH 1886

Following Hurricane Hugo, an extensive investigation of the courthouse documented the alterations made to the original building in the eighteenth and nineteenth centuries. Drawing by Willie Graham, Colonial Williamsburg Foundation, 1991.

periods survived, but each new renovation removed or severely altered the appearance and finishes of the early-nineteenth-century fabric.

In a way the courthouse is like a palimpsest, a document on which each generation since the late eighteenth century has fashioned its own cultural identity without, however, being able to completely erase the contributions of its predecessors. Yet, when the aspirations of an earlier age failed to meet those of a subsequent one, the resulting changes were often ruthless. Whereas colonial Charlestonians appreciated the symbolic importance of a grand staircase as a place of public spectacle, efficiency-minded Victorians despised the waste of space. Such conflicting perspectives have long shaped the image of public building in America. Grand buildings constructed with costly materials are sources of civic pride, providing a sense of community or national identity. However, the public expense that such structures engender invariably provokes outcries of wastefulness and calls for simple but very practical models. Public officials are often caught in the middle. They hope to erect something that reflects the values of their communities, but sentiment about public building often spans the spectrum of opinion. Low bids and short-term design programs ensure that public expenditures do not overly burden current budgets, but shoddy building and lack of vision often trigger even costlier cycles of repairs and rapid disenchantment with the way the structure functions. The architectural history of the Charleston County Courthouse is no less than the story of the struggle between these varying attitudes.

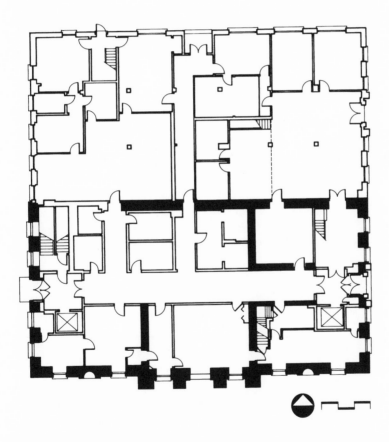

Plan of the Charleston County Courthouse, 1991. By the late twentieth century, numerous renovations and additions had turned the ground floor of the courthouse into a maze of corridors and offices, nearly obliterating the original plan and fabric. Drawing by Willie Graham, Colonial Williamsburg Foundation, 1991.

THE STATEHOUSE, 1753–1788

Charleston, the Provincial City

On 22 June 1753 James Glen, the royal governor of South Carolina, convened a meeting of the members of the King's Council and Commons House of Assembly to observe the anniversary of King George II's ascension to the throne with a grand ceremony. The crowning moment of the day occurred when these distinguished leaders of the colony gathered at the northwest corner of Broad and Meeting Streets in Charleston to lay the cornerstone of the first provincial statehouse. Those who gathered to witness the beginning of this undertaking no doubt observed the massive brick walls rising from the building site of St. Michael's Anglican Church catercorner to the statehouse lot and recalled a similar event the previous year. Following the ceremony Governor Glen and his entourage retired to John Gordon's tavern at the northeast corner of Broad and Church Streets for dinner, culminating in a number of toasts to celebrate the occasion.[4] As they drained the punch bowl, those giddily gathered in Gordon's long room spoke exultantly of the rising fortunes of the colony. In two bold steps taken within the space of sixteen months, Charleston proudly asserted its place as one of the leading cities of British America. In the heart of the city would soon rise a great basilican church and an imposing two-story statehouse.

These soaring sentiments of civic success soured over the next few years, as cost overruns and a chronic shortage of public funds sent legislators and vestrymen begging for money to complete these substantial projects. Originally estimated at £30,000, St. Michael's eventually cost twice that amount and was not completed until the early 1760s.[5] Work on the statehouse was not as agonizingly slow as on the church but still took a number of years to complete and faced the same escalating budget. Officials moved into the statehouse three years after the cornerstone had been laid, but the provincial court met in a room with bare brick walls until the late 1760s. Despite the protracted building process, members of the provincial government took great satisfaction in knowing that they had undertaken one of the grandest public buildings ever to be erected in the British American colonies. The new statehouse was a testament to the growing wealth and prestige of this southern colony, a sentiment obviously felt by Governor Glen when he asserted that "South

Portrait of James Glen (1701–1777). During Glen's lengthy tenure as royal governor, acts were passed by the assembly for the construction of the statehouse. Glen personally laid its cornerstone on 22 June 1753. Illustration provided by South Carolina Department of Archives and History, Columbia. Courtesy of the Earl of Dalhousie, Brechin, Scotland.

Carolina was perhaps more valuable to our Mother Country than any other Province on this Continent."[6]

For thirty-five years, until its destruction by fire in 1788, the statehouse was the center of South Carolina politics. It was in this building that imperial authority was asserted by the royal governors and boldly challenged by the Commons House of Assembly; that the momentous issues of national sovereignty were broached and the Declaration of Independence first proclaimed; and finally, in the 1780s, that the challenges of establishing a new form of government were passionately discussed and the federal constitution ratified.

The city of Charleston had grown rapidly in the quarter century leading up to the laying of the statehouse cornerstone. Much of the colonial culture that gave Charleston and the lowcountry such a distinctive character was largely a product of this period.[7] Political stability had been achieved when proprietary rule was overturned and replaced by royal authority in the 1720s. The ever-growing importation of African slaves provided the inexhaustible pool of labor needed to exploit the surrounding swamps, fields, and forests. As the plantation system matured during the 1730s, wealth flowed into the colony at an unprecedented level, in part generated by a dramatic increase in the production of rice. Once the British government lifted its ban on the export of rice to Iberian and Mediterranean ports, lowcountry planters aggressively opened up new markets for their crop.[8] The production of

8   indigo was introduced in the following decade and soon became the colony's second leading staple. By the 1750s these exports had made many planters among the wealthiest people in British North America.

Agricultural prosperity transformed the city of Charleston. The surge in staple exports was accompanied by the introduction of a variety of imported goods that soon turned luxury items into necessities. By midcentury, Charleston was the entre-pôt for this large and highly productive hinterland and had become a community where modest fortunes could be made by catering to the demands and needs of the planter plutocrats. Doctors, lawyers, school masters, and other professionals enriched the fabric of urban life, as men of taste and education found their skills and services in increasing demand. Merchants flocked to the city to establish wholesale and retail trade connections with firms in London, Bristol, and Glasgow, and subsidiary stores deep in the Carolina backcountry. Planters, provincial officials, and professionals found the city's shops filled with items ranging from imported ceramics, clothing, tea, and books to locally produced furniture, silverware, and coaches. Merchant James Crokatt boasted that he had "clothing, groceries, and textiles" newly arrived from London for those who desired to keep up with metropolitan fashions and tempted those who wanted to improve the appearance of their homes with "blue and red tiles for pavement, black and white marbles for hearths, and white or painted tiles for chimnies."[9] More and more ships docked at the wharves on the Cooper River, unloading exotic imported goods and taking on the rice, indigo, and lumber that underpinned the economic fortunes of the seaport and surrounding plantations.

Like few other cities, Charleston acted as a magnet, drawing the rich and powerful as well as the poor and enslaved. Besides the lure of consumer goods, planters were attracted to the city for many other reasons, not the least of which was the quest

Imported in Capt. *Pollixfen* from *London*, and to be fold by JAMES CROKATT, *great choice of fhoes for men, women and children, black pepper, all kind of fpices and citron, florence oyl in flasks or in bottles, flower of muftard, hair powder, corn-mills, rice-books, scotch plads, scotch and other forts of fowing-thread, fine chints, white and coloured callicoes, bed-ticks, damasks and many other fine filks, all kinds of linnen from the courfeft wrappers to the fineft cambrick, cheap bags for plantation use, and almoft every other kind of ufeful goods proper for this feafon: Alfo blue and red tiles for pavements, black & white marbles for hearths, and white or painted tiles for chimnies.*

Such perfons as have not yet paid or otherwife fatisfied the faid Crokatt for goods fold them before January laft, are defired to do it forthwith, in order to prevent trouble and expence to themfelves.

James Crokatt's advertisement for goods imported into Charleston included architectural stonework and ceramics. *South Carolina Gazette,* 9 August 1735, p. 4, col. 1.

Peter Manigault and Friends, 1754, by George Roupell. This wash drawing not only shows a number of prominent citizens who were intimately acquainted with the statehouse but is the only surviving contemporary depiction of the tavern culture of Charleston's elite in the eighteenth century. The dinner at Gordon's long room after the laying of the statehouse cornerstone would doubtless have looked much the same. Courtesy, Winterthur Museum, Winterthur, Delaware.

for political power. Clustered almost entirely in Charleston, the offices and courts of the provincial government so dominated the colony that few local institutions emerged that could serve as counterweights.[10] The way to power in South Carolina was not through the county court as in Virginia or Maryland but through a position in the provincial government or assembly-appointed local commissions.[11] More than any other British colony on the American mainland, Charleston functioned like an old medieval city-state.

Commerce and politics may have dominated the talk of taverns and dining rooms, but Charleston also provided its inhabitants and visitors with many social and cultural diversions. The pursuit of pleasure by the provincial elite spawned a host of new public activities and forms of entertainment. Theaters, music concerts, assemblies, balls, clubs, and other social events enriched the cultural life of the community. In 1773 a young Bostonian, Josiah Quincy, carefully recorded in his diary the details of a rich and active social world far more brilliant than that of his native city. Quincy spent much of his time dining in great houses, drinking fine wines,

10 toasting the beauties of the city, and talking politics. On other evenings he attended balls and assemblies, where he noticed the women and men "dressed with richness and elegance uncommon with us." On 17 March he "feasted with the Sons of St. Patrick. While at dinner six violins, two hautboys and bassoon [played]. . . . After dinner six French horns in concert—most surpassing musick!" Overwhelmed by the hospitality but wary of the many pleasures offered by Charleston society, Quincy observed that "state, magnificence and ostentation, the natural attendants of riches, are conspicuous among this people. . . . Cards, dice, the bottle and horses engross prodigious portions of time and attention; the gentlemen (planters and merchants) are mostly men of the turf and gamesters."[12] Public walks, assembly rooms, bathing houses, libraries, museums, theaters, and exhibitions provided places and opportunities for members of polite society to display their charms, beauty, and good breeding and to find suitable matrimonial partners. Over time, marriage alliances cemented the bond between planters, merchants, and professionals, creating a self-conscious elite society.

The concentration of wealth in the city naturally affected the habits of its citizens. As another eighteenth-century visitor observed:

> The manner of the inhabitants of Charleston are as different from those of the other North American cities as are the products of their soil. The profitable rice and indigo plantations are abundant sources of wealth for many considerable families, who therefore give themselves to the enjoyment of every pleasure and convenience to which their warm climate and better circumstances invite them. Throughout, there prevails here a finer manner of life . . . there were neither domestic circumstances to stand in the way nor particular religious principles, as among the Presbyterians of New England or the Quakers of Pennsylvania, to check the enjoyment of good living. So luxury in Carolina has made the greatest advance, and their manner of life, dress, equipages, furniture, everything denotes a higher degree of taste and love of show, and less frugality than in the northern provinces.[13]

One of the most striking manifestations of the new wealth of Charleston's merchants and planters was the investment in the reshaping and refining of the city's architectural fabric. A customary measure of a town's general prosperity in Britain and her American colonies was its physical form. Towns with an old fabric, few new buildings, or a lack of certain civic amenities were considered torpid or even on the decline while those busily engaged in tearing down or refacing old structures and putting up new buildings were viewed as thriving communities. In his survey of Great Britain in the 1720s, Daniel Defoe described the city of Worcester as an "old, though not very well built city . . . because the town is close and old, the houses standing too thick." In contrast he observed that in Somerset, the cloth-manufacturing town of Frome "is so prodigiously increased within these last twenty or thirty years, that they have built a new church, and so many new streets and houses . . . that it is very likely to be one of the greatest and wealthiest inland towns in England."[14]

View of Charles Town, 1739, engraving by W. H. Toms after a painting by Bishop Roberts. Detail shows public buildings that were used for important governmental functions before construction of the statehouse, including the Courtroom and Exchange at Tradd and East Bay Streets, and the Court of Guard with the council chamber above at Broad and East Bay Streets. Courtesy, Historic Charleston Foundation.

By these traditional indicators Charleston was a thriving seaport. As early as the 1720s the city was filled with houses of "Brick, Lime and Hair, and some very fine Timber Houses," most of which were "glazed with Sash Windows after the English Fashion."[15] At midcentury the city was in the midst of a thorough transformation. It had expanded considerably beyond the area enclosed by the fortified walls and moat, which had ringed the original city from the early 1700s until they were removed and filled in 1718. New streets extended northward up the peninsula and westward across to the low-lying lands along the Ashley River. Infilling in the area around White Point allowed the city to expand to the south as well. Developers laid out new boroughs with broad cross streets away from the old crowded areas along the Cooper River. Bishop Roberts's 1739 view of Charleston from the Cooper River depicts a densely packed urban scene with large dwellings, warehouses, and stores rising two and three stories. Along the waterfront wharves of Bay Street, storehouses and dwellings stretched three, five, and even ten bays in length. Some were pairs of row houses joined together under the same gable or gambrel roofs that ran parallel to the waterfront. Many buildings had cellars for storage, large ground-floor entrances into shops and storerooms, and second-story balconies that looked out across the Bay Street wharves to the river. In the old urban center and in the new developments on the periphery, brick, slate, and stucco had replaced wood as the materials of prestige. A fire in 1740 destroyed many blocks of buildings but provided the impetus to construct larger and more fireproof structures on the sites of old wooden tenements and shops.

12

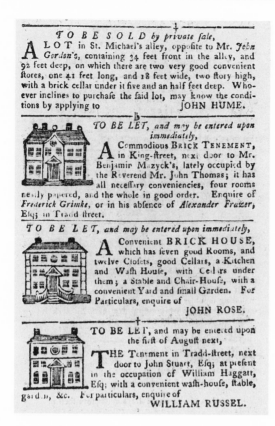

TO BE SOLD by private sale,

A LOT in St. Michael's alley, opposite to Mr. *John Gordon's*, containing 34 feet front in the alley, and 92 feet deep, on which there are two very good convenient stores, one 41 feet long, and 18 feet wide, two story high, with a brick cellar under it five and an half feet deep. Whoever inclines to purchase the said lot, may know the conditions by applying to JOHN HUME.

TO BE LET, and may be entered upon immediately,

A Commodious BRICK TENEMENT, in King-street, next door to Mr. Benjamin Mazyck's, lately occupied by the Reverend Mr. John Thomas; it has all necessary conveniencies, four rooms neatly papered, and the whole in good order. Enquire of *Frederick Grimke*, or in his absence of *Alexander Frazer*, Esq; in Tradd street.

TO BE LET, and may be entered upon immediately,

A Convenient BRICK HOUSE, which has seven good Rooms, and twelve Closets, good Cellars, a Kitchen and Wash House, with Cellars under them; a Stable and Chair-House, with a convenient Yard and small Garden. For Particulars, enquire of JOHN ROSE.

TO BE LET, and may be entered upon the first of August next,

THE Tenement in Tradd-street, next door to John Stuart, Esq; at present in the occupation of William Haggatt, Esq; with a convenient wash-house, stable, garden, &c. For particulars, enquire of WILLIAM RUSSEL.

Charleston newspapers in the late colonial period contained numerous advertisements for well-constructed brick dwellings. *South Carolina Gazette*, 25 June 1769. Courtesy, Charleston Library Society.

Because it was a port, Charleston had direct access to new architectural ideas promoted in design books, which were stocked by the city's booksellers, and in the buildings seen by the merchants and planters who frequented London, Bristol, and Glasgow on a regular basis. Pouring into the city as well were new materials, such as marble and mahogany, along with a steady stream of highly skilled British tradesmen who sought their livelihood in a prosperous, bustling community.[16] A number of canny craftsmen sought to capitalize on the desires of rich customers who wished to emulate the latest architectural fashions of England. In 1769 Ezra Waite, "Civil Architect, House-builder in general, and Carver, from London," advertised his expertise in the local newspaper, noting that he "has finished the architecture, conducted the execution thereof, viz. in the joiner way, all tabernacle frames (but that in the dining-room excepted) and carved all the said work in the four principal rooms; and also calculated, adjusted, and draw'd at large for to work by, the Ionick entablature, and carved the same in the front and round the eaves, of Miles Brewton, Esquire's House, on White Point." He appealed to wealthy Charlestonians that "if on inspection of the above mentioned work, and twenty-seven years experience, both in theory and practice, in noblemen and gentlemen's seats, be sufficient to recommend; he flatters himself to give satisfaction to any gentleman, either by plans, sections, elevations, or executions."[17]

ARCHITECTURE.

Ut res gesta est Narrabo Ordine,

EZRA WAITE,

Civil Architect, House-builder in general, and Carver,
from LONDON,

HAS finished the architecture, conducted the execution thereof, viz. in the joiner way, all tabernacle frames, (but that in the dining-room excepted) and carved all the said work in the four principal rooms; and also calculated, adjusted, and draw'd at large for to work by, the Ionick entablature, and carved the same in the front and round the eaves, of MILES BREWTON, Esquire's House, on *White-Point*, for Mr. MONCRIEFF.—If on inspection of the above mentioned work, and twenty-seven years experience, both in theory and practice, in noblemen and gentlemen's seats, be sufficient to recommend; he flatters himself to give satisfaction to any gentleman, either by plans, sections, elevations, or executions, at his house in *King-street*, next door to Mr. *Wainwright's*, where architecture is taught by a peculiar method never published in any book extant.

N. B. As MILES BREWTON, Esquire's dining-room is of a new construction, with respect to the finishing of windows and doorways, it has been industriously propagated by some, (believed to be Mr. *Kinsey Burden*, a carpenter) that the said WAITE did not do the architecture, and conduct the execution thereof. Therefore the said WAITE, begs leave to do himself justice in this public manner, and assure all gentlemen, that he the said WAITE, did construct every individual part, and drawed the same at large for the joiners to work by, and conducted the execution thereof. Any man that can prove to the contrary, the said WAITE promises to pay him One Hundred GUINEAS, as witness my hand, this 22d day of *August*, 1769.

Veritas odium parit.   EZRA WAITE.

The wealth of Charleston attracted skilled English craftsmen who found a ready audience in the merchants, planters, and professionals who had their principal residences in the city. London-trained builder Ezra Waite advertised his skills in the local newspaper. *South Carolina Gazette*, 22 August 1769. Courtesy, Charleston Library Society.

The Miles Brewton House, ca. 1769, King Street, Charleston. Often referred to as the "grandest Georgian townhouse surviving in America," this dwelling, as completed by a wealthy slave trader named Miles Brewton, reflected the craftsmanship available for Charleston buildings by the third quarter of the eighteenth century, from the stonework of its front portico and marble chimney pieces to the finely carved woodwork of its interior. Courtesy, Historic Charleston Foundation.

14   Charleston provided the opportunity to construct bold, new, classically inspired buildings on a scale that few other American cities could match. The planter elite of South Carolina, unlike their counterparts in Maryland and Virginia, chose to make Charleston their primary place of residence, electing to spend only short intervals of time on their country estates. Residing in town for extended periods, the great planters and their merchant suppliers maintained opulent urban residences, for it was here, in the city, that the notion of style mattered most. The rich materials and fine detailing of dwellings such as merchant Miles Brewton's house had few rivals elsewhere in the country. According to Josiah Quincy, Brewton's house was "said to have cost him 8000£ sterling" and contained, besides the carved woodwork of Ezra Waite, "the grandest hall I ever beheld, azure blue satin window curtains, rich blue paper with gilt, mashee borders, most elegant pictures, excessive grand and costly looking glasses etc."[18] It is no accident, then, that building in this city was more Anglicized, more substantial, and more embellished than in any other city in the entire South. A shift was occurring in architecture from vernacular construction to self-conscious classical design with a new approach to the layout and arrangement of the urban house lot. During this period Charlestonians settled upon a particular dwelling form that had its narrower gable end turned toward the street with one- and two-story piazzas stretching across the broad face of the building. Bishop Roberts's 1739 view of Charleston depicts few, if any, of these house types. Yet some fifty years later they had become so prevalent that Charlestonians commonly used the term "single house" as a shorthand reference for this distinctive building form.[19]

Investment in domestic architecture was matched by that in public building as Charlestonians asserted their communal and provincial identity in prominent and grand structures. In so doing, they were following an old pattern that had been established in British towns and cities where the erection of grand public structures became the means of affirming the ruling gentry's authority. Along with the desire to express a disinterested pride in a town's progress was the oligarchy's incentive to reinforce its own power over the rest of the inhabitants. Courts that were held in mean circumstances and assemblies that convened in makeshift quarters counte- nanced little respect, as Virginia legislators lamented in 1663, when they questioned "whether it was more profitable to purchase [a building for a statehouse] than to continue . . . with the dishonour of all our laws being made and our judgments given in alehouses" in Jamestown.[20] Visual signs played a key role and were increasingly linked to the dignity of office, both in general and personal terms. The market houses and town halls built throughout Britain's many market and shire towns in the seventeenth and eighteenth centuries are embellished with the emblematic inter- linking of private well-being and the public weal. Corporate arms found on civic maces, chairs, plate, and buildings are often intermingled with the personal coats of arms of benefactors, mayors, aldermen, and assemblymen, blurring the distinction between the officeholder and the office. The magistrates who undertook the con- struction of a new market hall in Leominster, Herefordshire, in the 1630s metaphor- ically expressed the relationship of power to building. Inscribed on the frieze of the timber-framed structure was the assertion that "like columnes do upprop the fabrik 15 of a building so noble gentri dos support the honour of a kingdom."[21]

The gentlemen responsible for the planning and construction of Charleston's public buildings understood this message implicitly. They sought to establish a physical coherence to the town by providing a civic center, a conspicuous place that drew together the various strands of the urban fabric. The placement of the statehouse and St. Michael's Anglican Church at the junction of Broad and Meeting Streets was no happenstance but a well-conceived piece of town planning. Earlier plans for the city had anticipated such a grand civic square at this location, but it had taken more than a half century of development before they were realized. The first Anglican church had been built on the southeast corner of the intersection in the late seventeenth century but had been replaced by St. Philip's Anglican Church further east on Church Street in the 1720s. The scheme envisioned in the Grand Model of Charleston by the Lords Proprietors in the 1680s was revived by the 1730s with the construction of a one-story brick market house for beef on the northeast corner of Broad and Meeting Streets, where the City Hall is now located. The massive size of the statehouse and St. Michael's Church, whose foundations had been laid one year earlier than the courthouse in 1752, created the requisite scale of a civic square. The area was complemented in the late 1760s by a two-story stuccoed treasury and

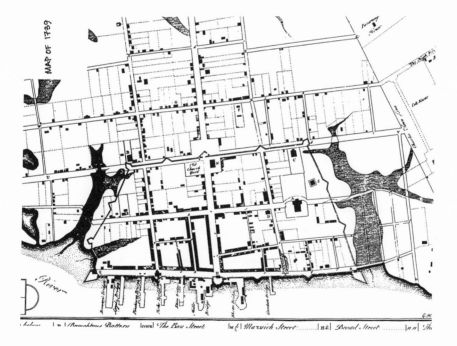

In this map of 1739, dedicated to Charles Pinckney, the draftsman depicted the spread of the city beyond the confines of its walls and the beginnings of the great public square at Meeting and Broad Streets envisioned in the grand model. The recently completed brick market appears on the northeast corner. Courtesy, Historic Charleston Foundation.

16   guardhouse with an "imposing pediment, supported by four massy pillars of the Tuscan order" facing north on the southwest corner of Broad Street.[22] Set several blocks distant from the crowded wharves and bustling alleys along the bay, the public square stood in the middle of the peninsula, perhaps as a bold assertion that Charleston would one day span the entire finger of land between the Ashley and Cooper Rivers. Removing important public functions from houses and buildings along the harbor to a more centralized location followed a pattern evident in other early American cities such as New York and Philadelphia, in which statehouses, city halls, hospitals, and churches were laid out on broad inland lots.

With construction of the statehouse, various bodies of South Carolina's government were housed together under one roof for the first time in the colony's history. Previously the provincial courts, council, secretary's office, and Commons House of Assembly had been spread throughout the town in houses, taverns, and smaller public buildings. The Commons House of Assembly had met for a number of years in a rented dwelling on Church Street. On occasion the provincial court held its sessions in the long room of a tavern at the northeast corner of Church and Broad Streets. At other times the court convened in a purpose-built, two-story structure that stood in the center of Bay Street at the termination of Tradd Street. Magistrates shared their building with merchants who frequented the exchange on the ground floor. One block to the north the governor and council had conducted their business on the upper floor of a two-story building just behind the Half Moon Bastion facing the harbor. Below the council chamber was the guardhouse, whose occupants kept a watchful eye on the surrounding docks, wharves, and taverns that crowded the harbor. Although the two buildings constructed for the council chamber and guardhouse and the courts and exchange were sited in conspicuous locations on the waterfront, their small scale and domestic appearance scarcely called attention to their public function.

The new statehouse provided a dramatic focus that had been missing when the various offices were dispersed across the city. Together with St. Michael's Anglican Church, which was built by many of the same craftsmen, the statehouse anchored one of the most impressive civic squares in colonial America. Not only did they provide a natural focal point among the mass of domestic structures and shops, but given their public nature, they were also seen to symbolize the prosperity and prestige of the entire community and province. The massive bulk of the statehouse also provided an appropriate setting for the formal rituals and ceremonial activities that permeated the public life of the colony, such as the proclamation of a new governor or monarch, the declaration of war, or the opening of the provincial courts. One such occasion occurred on 2 February 1761, when George III was proclaimed king. The ceremony began with:

> The regular troops commanded by lieutenant colonel [James] Grant, being marched down from the barracks, and drawn up in Broad Street (extending from the bay to the state-house) with the Charles Town regiment of militia, commanded by the hon. col. [Othniel] Beale, on their left; the artillery company, commanded by Capt. Robert Boyd, being assembled at Granville's bastion; the

Jacob Motte House, 69 Church Street. The Commons House of Assembly met in this dwelling before the construction of the statehouse. Courtesy, Historic Charleston Foundation.

Council House and Guard House. Detail from Bishop Roberts's painting of Charleston, ca. 1739. In this two-story structure, situated at the Half Moon Battery on Bay Street at the intersection with Broad Street, the council met in rooms on the second floor while the guard house below was reserved for the city watchmen. Courtesy, Colonial Williamsburg Foundation.

Brown bread 3 l.   Barbadoes Rum 11 s 3 d.

Advertisements.

Council Chamber, Aug. 8, 1735.

HIS Majesty's Honble Council having agreed to meet in the Council-Chamber on *Tuesday* the 2d of *Sept.* next, in order to hear & determine Caveats, all Persons concern'd are required to attend on that day : And such as have entered Caveats and shall not then appear to Support the same, their said Caveats shall be dismiss'd.

By Order of the Honble the Lieut. Governour and his Majesty's Honble Council.

JESSE BADENHOP, *C.C.*

WHereas the several Advertisements published in the Gazette of this Province, requiring

Notices of provincial meetings were announced in advance in the colony's newspaper. *South Carolina Gazette*, 2 August 1735. Courtesy, Charleston Library Society.

forts, the men of war, and all the merchant ships in the harbour having their colours displayed; about 11 o'clock his honour the Lieutenant Governor [William Bull] went from his own house to the State-house, attended by several gentlemen, the regulars and militia resting their arms all the while, and proclaimed the King in the council chamber. . . .

His Honour then came out of the Council Chamber, and walked into the square facing the state-house, preceded by the constables with their staves, William Murray Esq. pro deputy secretary and the hon. William Simpson Esq. chief justice (both on horseback) and the provost marshall carrying the sword of state, and followed by the members of his majesty's council, lieutenant colonel Grant, the commanders of his Majesty's Ships, public officers etc. where his Majesty was proclaimed a second time, Mr. Murray reading the proclaimation, and Mr. Simpson repeating it aloud, to which three huzzas succeeded. The procession then moved down Broad Street, opposite to the [old] Guard House, where the proclaimation was read, repeated, and followed by three huzzas as before. After this the regulars and militia marched by divisions to the bay, and drew up there, and the procession went on to Granville's bastion, where the king was proclaimed for the last time; immediately after which the cannon at Granville's, Craven's, and Broughton's bastions and fort Johnson were fired, followed by a general volley of small arms, and huzzaing was repeated twice more, by which time it was one o'clock, when the men of war and other vessels in the harbour likewise fired. His honour then returned to the state house where . . . he made a speech to the gentlemen present suitable to the solemn occasion. . . . In the evening many houses were illuminated, many loyal healths drank.[23]

Stately processions that marked ceremonies such as these generally began or ended at the statehouse. Less dramatic and more routine was the ceremony surrounding the quarterly opening of the provincial court. At the start of the August 1771 session of the Court of Common Pleas, many Charlestonians observed Chief Justice Thomas Knox Gordon, his assistant justices, court officers, and "the Gentlemen of the Law" walking in a formal "procession from his Honour's House in Queen Street to the Court-House."[24] Whether a formal procession or a trek from the hinterland, all roads converged upon the center of power and authority at the corner of Meeting and Broad Streets.

DESIGN

In many respects the design and function of the South Carolina Statehouse was similar to the public building tradition that flourished in the provincial towns of England. Since the restoration of the monarchy in 1660, dozens of public buildings

Chief Justice Thomas Knox Gordon, artist unknown, oil on canvas. Gordon, an Irish lawyer, arrived in Charleston in 1770 to take up his appointment as chief justice of the General Court. Considered a "royal placeman," Gordon served on the Governor's Council as well until forced to flee in 1777. He returned to Charleston from Belfast in 1780 during the British occupation and assumed many of his former duties in the occupied city by acting as head of the Board of Police. Courtesy, South Carolina State Museum, Columbia.

The County Hall, Aylesbury, Buckinghamshire, England, 1722–1740, Thomas Harris, architect. Photograph by Carl Lounsbury, 1984.

had been erected in English provincial towns to house law courts, government offices, markets, and assembly rooms.[25] British travelers visiting Charleston encountered a structure that resembled in form and scale the shire halls and assize courts found in such English towns as Exeter, Devizes, Nottingham, and Warwick. In contrast to the often ungainly and locally influenced designs of many colonial American courthouses and statehouses, the transatlantic antecedents of the South Carolina Statehouse are readily apparent in its Palladian-inspired form and classical details. They derive from a fundamental understanding of the rules of classical architecture, which were based on an elaborate system of proportioning and scaling one part in relationship to another and the application of the appropriate form and detailing of the constituent elements. Classical design created a hierarchy of forms that could be perceived by observing the relative size, richness, and relationship of various buildings, a facade, or parts of a building. The relative significance of a central doorway is demonstrated by its location and greater enrichment compared to those on either side; the importance of various floors in a building are indicated by the relative size of their windows—the larger they are, the more significant the space and activities within. The scale, form, massing, and detailing of such structures as the County Hall in Aylesbury, Buckinghamshire (1722–40), the Court House in Warwick (1725–28), the Guildhall in Worcester (1721–24), and the Exchange in Bristol (1741–43) provided Charlestonians with vivid images of civic architecture. Most were two or three stories tall and stretched from five to eleven bays in length with a massive door or projecting pediment usually accentuating the center of the building. Thoughtfully

The Court House, Warwick, Warwickshire, England, 1725–1730, Francis Smith, architect.
In the period between the Restoration and the beginning of the eighteenth century, countless
courthouses were constructed in the provincial towns of England. These buildings followed
a definable architectural vocabulary and were decorated with symbols of justice and Crown
authority. Their grand upper chambers provided space for not only judicial and governmental functions, but social ones as well. Photograph by Carl Lounsbury, 1990.

Statue of Justice, the Court House,
Warwick, Warwickshire. Symbols
of authority often decorated the
exterior of English civic buildings in
the eighteenth century. At the Court
House in Warwick, a gilded statue
of justice stands in a niche just
below the royal coat of arms and
above the main entrance into the
building. Photograph by Carl
Lounsbury, 1990.

22   conceived details—compass-headed windows, niches, cupolas, coats of arms, rustication, and arcades—provided these public buildings with a degree of architectural
sophistication that made them stand out as a source of local pride.

Although architectural pattern books and the creative minds of architects and
builders shaped many aspects of Charleston's architecture, the principal inspiration
for the South Carolina Statehouse design derived from these English public building
prototypes. How these forms were translated into a formal design for workmen to
follow on the building site remains unknown, since no drawings or specifications for
the statehouse's construction survive. As William Rigby Naylor's 1767 drawings for
the Exchange at the eastern end of Broad Street exemplify, there were a number of
master builders working in Charleston who were more than capable of devising a
plan and perhaps an elevation for the statehouse. Yet even drawings such as these do
not necessarily reveal the individual or source responsible for the design. It is more

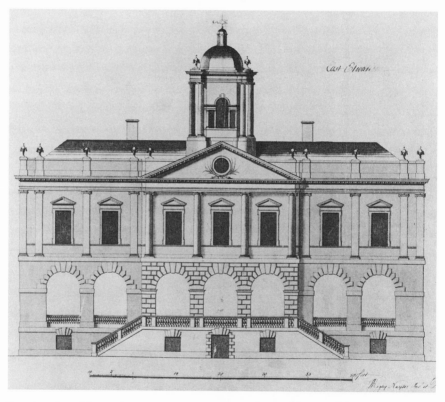

East elevation of the Exchange by William Rigby Naylor, ca. 1767. Skilled local draftsmen,
like Naylor, immigrated to eighteenth-century Charleston and, using their training as well as
English pattern books, shaped the architecture of Charleston between the fire of 1740 and
the American Revolution. The Exchange was constructed by skilled German undertakers
Peter Horlbeck and John Horlbeck, who had completed the privies and housekeeper's house
behind the statehouse by 1768. Courtesy, South Carolina Department of Archives and History, Columbia.

than likely that the actual design decisions emerged from the deliberations of a special building commission. When the assembly passed the act authorizing the construction of the statehouse on 14 June 1751, it named several men to direct its construction "with such Materials and of such Dimensions and with such useful Offices and necessary conveniences as to the said Commissioners shall seem needful and according to such plan or model as to them or the major part of them shall appear most conveniently and usefully to answer the Ends for which it is designed."[26]

Composed almost entirely of prominent members of the provincial assembly and Charleston merchants, the statehouse building commission simply appropriated recognizable architectural forms whose symbolic attributes would have been quickly understood in any part of the British empire. The commissioners included William Middleton, Charles Pinckney, William Bull, Jr., James Graeme, Andrew Rutledge, John Dart, Othniel Beale, Benjamin Smith, and Isaac Mazyck.[27] Middleton, Pinckney, and Bull served on the council. Smith and Dart sat as members of the Commons House, and Rutledge was the speaker of that body. Merchants Beale and Mazyck had been elected to the Commons House but declined to serve during the session. James Graeme, a friend of Governor Glen, was the colony's chief justice.[28] Many of these men had considerable experience in public and private building projects. For example, in the mid-1740s Charles Pinckney formulated a plan and estimated the costs of a grand two-story brick dwelling on Colleton Square facing the Cooper River. With its engaged pilastered portico and Venetian window lighting the stair landing at the back of the entrance hall, Pinckney's house was one of the first in the city to embody many of the English Palladian features that were to be repeated in the statehouse design. During the construction of part of the city's fortifications in

Miniature of Othniel Beale (1688–1773), artist unknown. Beale, a native of Marblehead, Massachusetts, prospered as a merchant in early eighteenth-century Charleston and served as a member and eventually as president of the Governor's Council and, in turn, on the select committee to oversee construction of the statehouse. Courtesy, Gibbes Museum of Art/Carolina Art Association, Charleston.

Isaac Mazyck (1700–1770). A prominent merchant and son of Huguenot immigrants, Mazyck served on many commissions during his long years of involvement in provincial government, which included the 1762 appointment to build a chapel of ease in St. James, Goose Creek Parish. Courtesy, Gibbes Museum of Art/Carolina Art Association, Charleston.

Pinckney mansion, Colleton Square, Charleston. This post Civil War photograph records the shell of the house of Charles and Eliza Lucas Pinckney, completed a decade before the laying of the cornerstone for the statehouse. The dwelling burned in a fire that swept through Charleston in 1861. The surviving specifications and documentation indicate its ambitious scale, and the engaged columnar portico would seem to be a precedent for the statehouse's original elevation. Pinckney served as a commissioner for its construction. Courtesy, Library of Congress, Washington, D.C.

the early 1750s, another statehouse commissioner, merchant Othniel Beale, devised a system of piles and rafts to carry the weight of ramparts over boggy marshes. Beale may have used his engineering experience with the ramparts once again when it came to laying the foundations of the statehouse over the unstable ground formed by the fill of the former moat that had surrounded the city in the early part of the eighteenth century.[29] Finally, on the same day that they were appointed as statehouse building commissioners, seven of the nine members were also appointed to oversee the construction of St. Michael's Church.[30] Thus Pinckney, Bull, Graeme, Rutledge, Beale, Smith, and Mazyck not only were familiar with each other's building experience but also were to gain full knowledge of the talents of Charleston craftsmen needed to undertake these monumental projects.

No account or minutes of the deliberations of the building commissioners survive, so it is difficult to ascertain the precise role of each member or to suggest whether one of them or some other individual was responsible for the overall design of the structure.[31] Throughout most of the American colonies in the late colonial period, the design of public buildings was often the result of collective decisions. Generally a committee would decide upon the overall size, plan, number of stories, materials, and placement of doors and windows with the details developed in consultation with the builder (or undertaker, as he was known in the eighteenth century). Alternatively a committee member or an undertaker may have submitted drawings to the group, consisting of a plan and perhaps one or two elevations. The committee then accepted or reworked the proposals. In such instances the design might result in novel solutions devised by an individual who had traveled, or who had access to builders' books, or who understood the latest architectural fashions from experience in the building trades. In most cases designs submitted by individuals simply followed familiar patterns. After the overall design scheme was settled, secondary decisions were made about the finishes of doors, windows, and walls and types of cornices and stairs, leaving the details of execution more or less in the hands of the professional builders and individual craftsmen who carried out their work in the customary fashion of the city or region.

Built of brick and covered with stucco by 1768, the statehouse was a two-story structure of nine bays with a pedimented central pavilion on the south facade.[32] The east and west elevations extended five bays along Meeting Street and Statehouse Alley, respectively. Stepped footings extending more than six feet below the current street grade provided support for the two-story walls.[33] A large doorway marked the center bay of each of these sides. A hipped roof probably covered the building although no physical or documentary evidence of this survives. The dominant feature of the main, south front was a three-bay pedimented projection. This feature was shallower and slightly narrower than the present pavilion although its precise configuration remains uncertain. In 1763 Dr. George Milligen Johnston, a Charleston physician, described the center bays as "decorated with four 2/3 Columns of the Composite Order, whose Capitals are highly finished, supporting a large angular Pediment and Cornice."[34] Obscured by subsequent rebuilding, these

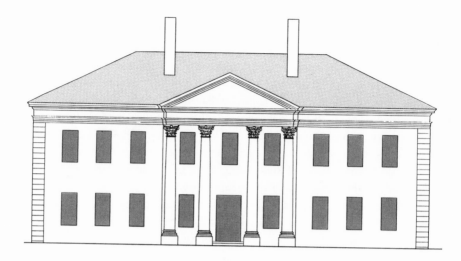

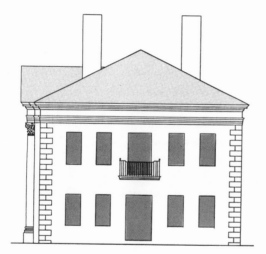

Conjectural elevation of the South Carolina Statehouse. Although it was generally known that the statehouse was two stories high, with a front portico of composite order columns, evidence for the ground level of the portico and the original position and size of the windows was discovered in the investigation. Drawing by Mark R. Wenger, Colonial Williamsburg Foundation.

four engaged Composite order columns probably stood at grade rather than on a
plinth and extended two full stories in height.[35]

In the overall design there was little to distinguish the statehouse from the formulaic pattern of public and country house architecture that had flourished in Great Britain for more than a quarter century. In this broader context the severely plain, two-story rectangular block set off in the center by a projecting three-bay pediment fit comfortably into prevailing English architectural fashion that has been labeled Palladian. Only the absence of a rusticated ground floor and the lack of carved or molded detailing around the apertures marked the structure as a modest, provincial interpretation of metropolitan taste. Yet in the context of the American colonies, it was indeed a landmark, heralding a more sophisticated application of design ideas in public building. Few other colonies could boast of a structure of such scale and form—an achievement that projected a clear image of the cultural aspirations of the province.

Enough physical evidence has survived in various locations to suggest the general treatment of the door and window openings in the building. The original window frames sat behind brick jambs, as was typical for London buildings of the period but rarely seen in the colonies. The recessed window frames of the statehouse reflected an English fashion that had grown out of building regulations introduced in the late seventeenth and early eighteenth centuries to help retard the spread of fire. The statehouse openings were a few inches higher than the present lintel height and decoratively crowned by flat arches of rubbed and gauged brickwork. These finely worked flat arches were subsequently covered with stucco in the 1760s. As with many buildings in Charleston and the surrounding lowcountry, such as St. James Goose Creek, this covering of carefully executed brickwork leads one to question whether the statehouse was intended to be roughcast from the outset or changing fashion rendered the skilled craftsmanship of the bricklayer superfluous. Certainly at a later date, damage from earthquakes, fires, hurricanes, and wars forced many residents to stucco their brick walls in order to hide the repairs.

The removal of stucco from the lower stories of the courthouse revealed the position of the original brick jack arches of the colonial statehouse. The decorative rubbed and gauged bricks forming the arch over a ground-floor window on the east wall remained exposed for a decade before the entire building was stuccoed in the 1760s. The statehouse windows were slightly higher and between four and eight inches to one side of the present 1792 openings. Photograph by Willie Graham, Colonial Williamsburg Foundation, 1993.

28   Perhaps more importantly, eighteenth- and early-nineteenth-century fashion provided another incentive to render brickwork with a covering, sometimes from the
outset. Stucco and Roman cement were less expensive means of imitating stone, a
more prestigious material, and Charlestonians certainly took to this trend with
great zeal, as an Englishman noted in a visit to the city in 1774. The statehouse, St.
Michael's Church, and the guardhouse were "plaistered over so well on the outside
to imitate stone that I really took them all for stone buildings at first." Both Broad
and Meeting Streets contained "many large handsome modern built brick houses
also some of brick inside and plaistered over on the outside so as to imitate stone
very well."[36]

On the interior the statehouse windows had seats raised approximately four-
teen inches above the floor. Structural evidence reveals that all fenestration from this
period had straight lintels and was not arched on the exterior.[37] The two ground-
floor openings flanking the Broad Street entrance were never doorways but flat-
headed windows with no quoins or decorative stonework. The sash, door and
window architraves, and other details probably resembled those still found in surviving Charleston buildings of the period, such as St. Michael's church. As was typical of Charleston and the rest of America in the late colonial period, wide,
quarter-round, molded muntins divided individual panes of clear English crown
glass; doors of four, six, and sometimes eight raised panels hung on wooden jambs;
and single and double architraves with bold ovolo and cyma moldings framed apertures. At midcentury, raised-panel wainscoting, accentuated at the dado level by
molded surbases, often festooned entire rooms or parts of them although Charleston
was beginning to develop the penchant for a flat-paneled type. Although this woodwork certainly appeared in many of the more important rooms of the statehouse,
just how pervasive it was remains unknown.

GROUND-FLOOR PLAN

The commissioners who designed and oversaw the construction of the statehouse in
the 1750s intended the building to match the political and cultural ambitions of a
wealthy and sophisticated society of merchants and planters. Although the cost of
construction stretched the colony's financial resources—already burdened by the
escalating price of defending the backcountry in an imperial war—and slowed the
completion of the interior fittings for many years, the commissioners never wavered
in their determination to provide the colony with a grand building.[38] In 1756 they
attempted to squeeze more money from the Commons House of Assembly to complete the interior, firmly believing that "the Dimensions will not be thought too
large, or the Ornaments, with which it is proposed to be decently embellish'd, superfluous, when the flourishing Condition of this Province is considered."[39] The commissioners almost literally had been pouring appropriated funds down a hole in an
effort to secure a firm foundation for the building. Builders had to sink piles to support the stepped footings of the statehouse foundations since it partly rested on fill
from a section of the earlier moat.[40]

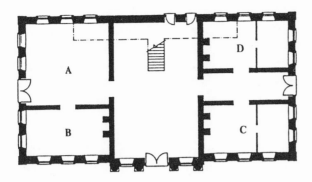

FIRST FLOOR PLAN

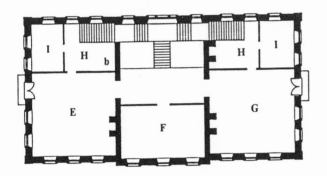

SECOND FLOOR PLAN

A. Courtroom
B. Magistrates' Room and/or Jury Room
C. Secretary's Office
D. Housekeeper's Apartments
E. Commons House of Assembly
F. Speaker's Chamber
G. Council Chamber
H. Lobby
I. Clerk's Office

b. Possible location of stair to attic armory

Conjectural plan of the statehouse, 1753–1788. Measured by Mark R. Wenger, Carl R. Lounsbury, Willie Graham, and W. Brown Morton III. Drawing by Willie Graham, Colonial Williamsburg Foundation, 1991.

30   The plan of the new statehouse provided spaces in which to gather, converse, and deliberate—rooms consonant with the political structure of the colony. A generous part of the ground floor was given over to circulation. A pair of transverse brick walls running northward from the corners of the front pavilion once divided the statehouse into three roughly equal parts. Portions of both walls still survive on the lower floor. Although the northern half of the west wall has been demolished, a patch of reworked and cut bricks on the back north wall and broken corners at the end of the present east corridor reveal that these cross walls were continuous. However, it seems likely that they were pierced by openings at their mid-points.

The middle third of the building, corresponding with the central pavilion of the Broad Street front, was the primary entry into the statehouse. This space ran the entire depth of the building, with a large stair rising on the rear wall. It was here that assemblymen and councilors gathered to discuss issues before they ascended the stair leading to their respective chambers. As in many English courts, the lobby also provided a sheltered space for dozens of lawyers, litigants, and spectators to meet to review court strategy or to exchange the latest political and social gossip before entering the provincial courtroom, housed in the large northwest room. As was typical of grand lobby entrances in English shire halls and assembly rooms, this central space was probably paved with imported stones.[41] Although the physical evidence has disappeared, its quite likely that a door or an arched opening on the west transverse wall near the center of the building provided access to the lower end of the courtroom. In many British shire halls as well as the statehouse in Philadelphia, the back of the courtroom was not closed off by a door but remained open directly into a hall or corridor. At the Charleston statehouse, another opening opposite the courtroom entrance communicated with a corridor that led to the secretary of the colony's office and the housekeeper's apartment in the eastern section of the ground floor.

Evidence for the original configuration of the grand staircase is slight. No pockets in the brick walls for stair framing have been found, possibly an indication that the landings were initially supported from below. What is known about the original stair has been deduced from the survival of early window apertures on the rear wall, door openings in the transverse walls, and a 1765 description of the statehouse. On the basis of that evidence, it appears that the lower flight began its ascent along the central axis of the entry, rising to a landing on the back wall.[42] Just above this landing a broad masonry opening with an elliptical head undoubtedly framed a three-part aperture division known as a Venetian window. Shaped perhaps like its contemporary in the chancel of St. Michael's church, this impressive feature provided a visual focal point for the space while illuminating the stair and the second-floor passage. Higher on the back wall, nearly abutting the cross walls, were two circular-headed windows that once lit stair landings in each corner.

At the great Venetian window the stair split and ascended to these corner landings along the rear wall of the entry hall. From each of the corner landings, a large opening in the transverse wall allowed the stair to continue its ascent along the rear wall, reaching the second floor about thirteen feet beyond the transverse wall. One

Central portion of the north wall on the second floor. The doorway to the left is in the location of the original Venetian window (note the arch near floor level). The window to the right was inserted in 1883 when the central stair was removed. All plaster on the upper run of the stair dates from the 1788–1883 period. The ghost of the paneling on the upper run of the stair is visible between the two windows, partially defined by the plaster. Photograph by Willie Graham, Colonial Williamsburg Foundation, 1991.

South staircase, St. Michael's Church, Charleston. St. Michael's, diagonally across the street, was authorized for construction by the Commons House of Assembly at the same time as the statehouse. Although completed a few years after the statehouse in 1762, St. Michael's was undoubtedly the work of many of the same craftsmen who had constructed the statehouse. The original balustrade of this stair may indicate the style of that formerly in the lobby of the statehouse. Photograph by Willie Graham, Colonial Williamsburg Foundation, 1986.

32   flight landed in a lobby area in the eastern section of the building, which led to the
council chamber; the other flight provided similar access to the western part of the
building, where the Commons House of Assembly met. This configuration con-
forms to a description made by a visitor who saw the statehouse in 1765: "There
are two flights of stairs, one leading to the Council Chamber, the other to the assembly room."[43] Thus the long-standing formal separation of the two legislative bodies
received explicit architectural recognition in two separate second-floor stairs.
Directly above the Venetian window was a smaller window, perhaps capped by a
compass head that lit the second-floor passage between the assembly room and
council chamber.

The rear wall of the ground-floor entry bears evidence for several periods of
changes, as windows were converted to doors and vice versa. Since much of this wall
has been disturbed by later additions and apertures, it is difficult to determine the
number and location of these early doors.[44] The chronological and functional relationship of these doors is problematic. Initially there may have been only two doors
exiting the rear of this space. By the end of the eighteenth century, there were at least
three. Evidence for a possible fourth door, just west of center on the rear wall, was
destroyed by subsequent alterations made during twentieth-century renovations.
The explicit purpose of these various doors remains enigmatic, but they did provide
convenient access to the rear yard from the entry hall. The multiple entries suggest

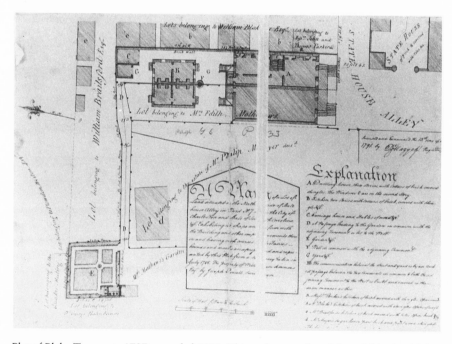

Plat of Blake Tenement, 1787, recorded 1791. This real estate plat of the neighboring Blake
Tenement depicts the outbuildings and gates at the rear of the statehouse along Statehouse
Alley. McCrady Plat Collection, Charleston County Register of Mesne Conveyance Office.

Late-nineteenth-century view showing the housekeeper's (jailer's) house and the west privy at the back of the statehouse lot. These buildings and the east privy, which was demolished in the mid-1880s, were built by the Horlbeck brothers by the late 1760s. Courtesy, Charleston Museum, Charleston.

that the rear yard may have been subdivided by fences, but any evidence for these divisions was obliterated with the subsequent additions built over the yard.[45] Alternatively some of these apertures may have been windows that would have provided light for the rear portions of the stair entry.

If there were no subdivision of the rear courtyard, the space may have provided convenient access for those who traveled to the statehouse by carriage or coach. The removal of twentieth-century additions to the building in 1993 revealed the foundations of a ten-by-forty-foot, barrel-vaulted chamber covered by a paved platform that stretches across the center of the north wall. Probably dating from the late eighteenth or early nineteenth century rather than the colonial statehouse period, it served as a cistern since it was submerged entirely below grade and was lined with stucco. This may have been the feature referred to in 1877 and 1878, when bills were submitted for repairing and cleaning the cistern and flagstone "in the courthouse yard."[46] With its paved floor above the barrel vault, this feature probably provided a more formal entrance into the back of the building and may possibly help explain the presence of so many apertures piercing the center section of the north wall.[47]

By 1768 an unspecified number of outbuildings lying north of the statehouse had been constructed by Peter and John Horlbeck.[48] At the time of the fire in February

Civil War era view of Meeting Street looking south. Depicted in this view is the east privy and northeast elevation of the courthouse. Courtesy, New-York Historical Society, New York.

1788, three brick buildings (two privies and a two-story housekeeper's or messenger's house, later converted into a jailer's house) stretched along the north boundary of the statehouse property. These buildings, together with a brick wall, enclosed the rear yard.[49] The privies were one story in height, had quoins at their corners, and were capped by pyramidal roofs. Two large gate piers stood near the center of both the east and west walls, allowing access into the courtyard. Footpaths paved with stone ringed the outside of the courtyard wall on the west, north, and east sides. Within the yard were one or more pumps covering wells.[50] Archaeological testing of the courtyard uncovered another cistern—a small, circular, domed structure—near the northwest privy, but evidence of the wells proved elusive.[51]

The two flanking sections of the statehouse varied significantly from the entry hall and thus reflected their distinct functions. The western third of the building was probably divided into two rooms of unequal size. Removal of plaster around the west entrance revealed ambiguous evidence as to whether there was originally a longitudinal brick partition north of the door. On the south side of this opening, though, a vertical band of roughly chopped brickwork indicated that a wall once existed in this location. If there were no wall north of the west entrance, this southern wall created a large square room in the northwest corner of the building—the ground-floor courtroom mentioned in the early descriptions of the building. It seems likely that this courtroom had two entrances. One of these was an exterior door located at the center of the building's west facade. A segmental arch and wood lintel once spanned this eight-foot opening, indicating that it initially had a flat head.[52]

With the destruction of the transverse wall in a subsequent renovation, evidence for a fireplace heating this space has also disappeared although it seems likely that a fireplace once stood in this position. However, the absence of a fireplace would not have been unusual since most early courtrooms in England and America remained unheated until the early nineteenth century. To maintain the symmetrical balance of chimneys, a false stack may have risen above the roofline of the statehouse. False chimneys appeared in such important eighteenth-century buildings as Nomini Hall, the home of Robert Carter in Westmoreland County, Virginia. It is clear from physical evidence that a chimney stack did rise from the ground floor through the northwest section of the building after the 1788 fire.[53]

Little is known about the original courtroom furnishings. As late as 1765, complaints were made about the unfinished appearance of the room, especially the fact that no plaster had been applied over the bare brick walls.[54] In 1768 Thomas Coleman was paid £160.17.6 for curtains and "sundry work for the courtroom."[55] No doubt the room contained a raised dais with a table and chairs or a bench for the chief magistrate and his associates, perhaps located near the north wall; a clerk's table; and one or two long benches arranged with railings to form a lawyers' bar. Part of the courtroom may have been paved with imported stones, as was typical of many courtrooms in Virginia during the late colonial period.[56]

In the absence of a county court system until the 1770s, Charleston was the center of a highly centralized legal system. The Court of Common Pleas met quarterly—in February, May, August, and November—and brought citizens from throughout the colony to the halls and courtroom of the statehouse. The court must have been a lively place during the few dramatic moments that punctuated the more common routine of the docket. In 1771 the trial of Dr. John Haly, accused of murdering Peter De Lancey in a duel, attracted "the most crowded Audience that ever was assembled there upon any Occasion." The jury returned a verdict of manslaughter, and Haly escaped with his life, due in no small part to the skills of his legal counsel, James Parsons, Thomas Heyward, Charles Cotesworth Pinckney, and Alexander Harvey. As the newspaper noted, the last three lawyers were "Natives of this Province, and lately from the Temple [one of the English Inns of Court], who acquired no small Degree of Applause by their Pleading upon this Occasion."[57]

By the time of the Haly trial, more than two dozen lawyers practiced before the magistrates in this room. The bar was a mixture of immigrants, such as Irishman James Parsons, and natives who had studied law in Charleston or had been formally trained in London.[58] Many were to use the skills first learned in legal argument in the courtroom to persuade and command influence in the political debates that emanated from the provincial assembly chamber upstairs. Although the case load

36

Summons, March 1786. In this summons William Cameron is called to serve as a juryman at a Court of Common Pleas "at the State-House, in Charleston." Courtesy, South Carolina Historical Society, Charleston.

before the provincial court doubled from the 1750s to the 1760s, the number of lawyers increased only slightly. As Lt. Gov. William Bull observed in 1770, this may have been due to the fact that South Carolinians relied overwhelmingly on just a few individuals, such as Parsons, Pinckney, and John Rutledge. He noted that five or six members of the bar argued more than half the cases that came before the Court of Common Pleas.[59]

A smaller room in the front west corner of the building opened into the south end of the courtroom through a door in the east-west partition. Examination of the wall shared by the entrance hall revealed that there was no direct access from the central section of the building until 1883. Before that, one reached this space by passing through the courtroom, an arrangement suggesting that the smaller space served either as a jury or magistrates' room. The fireplace on the east wall of this chamber, removed during the 1883 renovations, provided warmth to the judges and jurors who deliberated in this space, a typical provision accorded jury and magistrates' rooms in eighteenth-century American courthouses.

The eastern third of the building had a lateral corridor, running from the Meeting Street entrance to another door opening into the central lobby. The corridor bisected this part of the lower floor into two equal-sized apartments. The resulting spaces may have been further subdivided during the statehouse period, for, in addition to the courtroom, Johnston's 1763 description mentioned the secretary of the colony's office and "Apartments for the House-keeper" on the ground floor.[60] The term "apartments" suggests that the housekeeper's area, possibly in the northeast space, consisted of more than one room. In the colonial Virginia town of

Williamsburg, for example, the public gaoler and professors at the College of William and Mary enjoyed quarters made up of two rooms. Both the northeast and southeast spaces were heated by fireplaces located on the eastern transverse wall. One problem that the physical evidence presents is the fact that the doors opening into these two spaces from the longitudinal corridor each measures nearly six feet in width. This would suggest that one entered both spaces through double doors, a perfectly logical solution for the entrance into the secretary's office but one more problematic for the entrance into the subservient space provided for the house-keeper. Perhaps the designers wished to maintain the symmetry of the openings since they were placed opposite one another in the corridor.

The southeast room housed the office of the secretary of the colony. This too could have been subdivided by a frame partition, but as the original framing was entirely destroyed in the fire of 1788, it is impossible to be certain how these spaces were first configured. However, a documentary reference indicates that the secretary's office was subdivided in some manner. In 1758 Secretary John Murray was more than a little dismayed to observe that the "apartments intended for the Secretarys Office" were "neither fitted up in so decent or Commodious a Manner as an Office of such Consequence ought to be, and as the Reputation of the Province and the Safety of the Writing requires, for although the Rooms are in themselves sufficiently Large and Spacious yet there is not one Press or Closet for the Records in the Whole."[61] These deficiencies were partly rectified a few months later, when the cabinetmaking firm of Thomas Elfe and Thomas Hutchinson was paid for "making a Book Case for the Use in the Secretary's Office."[62]

SECOND-FLOOR PLAN

Physical evidence for the original arrangement of the second floor is scant. All original framing perished in the 1788 fire, and the brick transverse walls were demolished above the second-floor joists in 1883. Still, documentary sources offer some valuable clues as to how this space was furnished and how it functioned. The two principal legislative bodies met in large rooms located in the eastern and western front sections of the structure. The council chamber and the Commons House of Assembly room each had its own stair, lobby, and clerk's office. The commissioners of the building must have had in mind two spaces of comparable size and configuration when they first laid out the plan of the building, for, in March 1756 the Commons House asked Gov. James Glen and the council to "make choice of such Rooms therein as they shall think most convenient for their reception."[63] Johnston described the layout of the upper floor as consisting of "two large, and handsome Rooms; one is for the Governor and Council, the other for the Representatives of the People, with lobbies and rooms for their clerks."[64] Another observer remarked in 1765 that the two principal rooms were each about forty feet square.[65] Actually the rooms could not have been larger than about thirty-two feet square since the two transverse walls originally divided the upper floor into thirds as below. In all likelihood the two larger rooms were located on the front of the building since the symmetrical flights of stairs that

38   rose to each chamber landed at the back of the building on the rear wall. The mention of lobbies to the two chambers might refer to small circulation spaces at the top of each run with clerk's offices adjoining although this would mean that the lobbies and not the clerk's offices would have been heated. Entrance into the thirty-two-foot-square chambers would have been through a door in a framed partition.

Between the two main rooms a railed gallery overlooking the main stair may have connected the chambers of the council and assembly. In the remaining space between the two rooms was the "Speaker's Chamber," which probably functioned as a committee room used by the speaker of the Commons House of Assembly.[66] This space may have been heated by two fireplaces opposite one another on the transverse partition walls.

The equal size of the two legislative chambers belies what was actually a marked contrast in the relative authority of the two bodies. Once a strong force in provincial politics, the council lost much of its power to the lower house in the third quarter of the eighteenth century. The Commons House controlled the purse strings of the provincial treasury and made the most of its prerogative in financial matters, accumulating power at the expense of the governor and the upper house.[67] Although the locus of authority was in the Commons House, the furnishing of the two principal chambers suggests that the governor and council still played a vital role as the king's chief officers in the colony. After all, many routine affairs of state brought hundreds of citizens into this room that served as the governor's office. In the late 1750s Gov. William Henry Lyttelton reserved the space for "every Friday at eleven o'clock in the forenoon, for proving of wills, and qualifying executors and administrators."[68] Perhaps most importantly it was in the council chamber that the king's authority was acknowledged and important proclamations were first read by the governor.[69] Even after the overthrow of colonial government, state officials continued the tradition of observing important occasions in the council chamber. On the first anniversary of the Declaration of Independence, "an elegant Entertainment was given at the Council-Chamber by his Excellency the President [of the Privy Council, John Rutledge] to such Members of the Legislature as were in Town, to the Clergy, civil and military Officers, and a number of other Gentlemen. After Dinner . . . Thirteen Toasts were given."[70]

The statehouse designers further accentuated the symbolic role of the council chamber in provincial affairs by creating a ceremonial balcony on the Meeting Street facade. Public officials stepped through a broad central doorway onto a railed balcony above the east entrance below. Echoing a similar appendage on the second-floor level of the old council chamber and guardhouse building on East Bay Street and an integral feature of other contemporary public buildings (such as the statehouse in Boston, the Colony House in Newport, and the capitol in Williamsburg), the South Carolina Statehouse balcony provided a dramatic venue for important events, such as the proclamation of a new king, governor, or system of government.[71]

Following two-and-half tumultuous years of occupation of Charleston by the British army, the South Carolina legislature reconvened in the old statehouse in early

1783 and in February elected Charleston lawyer and planter Benjamin Guerard as 39
the new governor. In order to reestablish their authority and confirm their legitimacy,
members of the House of Representatives (the old Commons House of Assembly)
authorized "that his Excellency the Governor be proclaimed with the usual Ceremonies from the Balcony of the Senate Room."[72] Although the names of the legislative bodies and the allegiance of the government may have changed, the new order
easily appropriated the forms and symbols of the old colonial government.[73]

Important ceremonies of state required the proper fittings to accord with their
solemnity. As a result, in the late 1750s and early 1760s the council chamber was
elaborately finished with woodwork and furniture thought to "be suitable and
proper for the rooms in the State House . . . occupied by the Governour and Council."[74] Although £25,000 had been appropriated in 1751 for the construction of the
statehouse and an additional £12,500 levied in 1757, those supervising the construction continued to push for more money to hire some of the best craftsmen in
Charleston, many of whom were later among the most active mechanics in the drive
for American independence.[75] Overlooking the intersection of Broad and Meeting
Streets, in the eastern section of the statehouse, the council chamber was ringed with
sixteen wooden Corinthian pilasters carved by Thomas Woodin out of what may
have been white pine imported from New England. Woodin, a London carver who
had immigrated to Charleston in the early 1760s, was paid £471.18.0 for his hand-
iwork.[76] Prominently located in this elaborately paneled room were the armorial
bearings of the monarch, which had been carved by Philadelphia craftsman
Nicholas Bernard. The carver arrived in Charleston in the fall of 1765 and advertised in the *South Carolina Gazette* that among the items he had for sale was "the
King's Coat-of-Arms carved in wood, suitable for a State House or Court-House."[77]
Bernard's timely or calculated appearance in town netted him more than £73 from
the Commons House for his carving.[78] Perhaps hanging nearby was the portrait of
King George, which was ceremonially draped with a curtain made by upholsterer

Coat of arms of George III,
carved, gilded wood. This set
of arms is much like that
acquired from Philadelphia
carver Nicholas Bernard for
the council chamber of the
statehouse. Courtesy, Colonial
Williamsburg Foundation.

Hand and coronet, oil on canvas, ca. 1740. In 1883 the Charleston City Council was presented with this fragment of a portrait of a British queen that formerly hung in the statehouse. Portraits of Queen Anne and George I or Queen Caroline and George II are known to have been in the building before their removal in the American Revolution. The National Portrait Gallery, London, believes this fragment to be taken from a painting of Queen Caroline by court painter Jervas. Collection of City Hall, Charleston.

Edward Weyman, one of the leading radical artisans in Charleston. Additional portraits of the royal family and other notables also may have been placed on the walls of the room.[79] Warming the councilors as they deliberated on cool winter days was a fireplace decorated with an expensive stove grate.[80]

Furniture in the room probably consisted of a table covered with broadcloth, as was typical of courtrooms and statehouses throughout the American colonies and England, and a set of chairs for the twelve councilors. Charleston cabinetmakers Thomas Elfe and Thomas Hutchinson, makers of the book press in the secretary's office, were paid £728.2.6 in 1758 for "chairs and tables in the Council Chamber."[81] A mahogany chair with carved feet and arms, reputedly the royal governor's chair from the council chamber, survives in Columbia and has been attributed to this shop.[82] Such a ceremonial chair would certainly have been in keeping with the rest of the robustly carved woodwork in the room. Finally, for a short period a bar just within the entrance into the room symbolically prohibited those who were not specially invited into the council chamber. This traditional feature found in courtrooms and in state bedchambers of kings and noblemen was removed by order of the Commons House in 1761, perhaps out of a spiteful regard for its own prerogative.[83]

Packed into a room measuring no more than thirty-two by thirty-two feet, the richness of the furnishings and fittings in the council chamber could not have failed to impress visitors, though not always uncritically. In 1763 Johnston thought that the room appeared "rather crouded and disgusting, than ornamented and pleasing, by the great Profusion of carved Work in it."[84] Two years later Pelatiah Webster

Governor's chair. The ambitious scale of this chair has accentuated the proposition that it served as the governor's ceremonial seat in the council chamber in the statehouse. As the noted cabinetmaking firm of Elfe and Hutchinson provided all of the furnishings for the council chamber in 1758, it probably made this piece, the only item from the room to survive. Courtesy, South Caroliniana Library, University of South Carolina, Columbia.

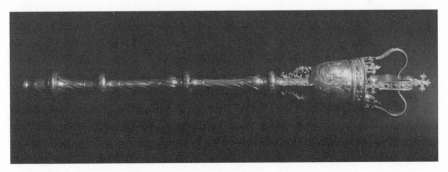

Mace. The official mace for the royal colony of South Carolina was made in London in 1756 by Magdalen Feline of gilded silver. It includes the royal coat of arms and three other devices. Josiah Quincy described its use in the statehouse and in processions in his journal in 1773. Recovered after the American Revolution, it is still used by the South Carolina General Assembly. Courtesy, South Carolina General Assembly. Photograph by Bruce Flashnick, Columbia.

House of Commons, London. Engraving by B. Cole. This image depicts a session of the British House of Commons. The seating of members, the speaker (with hat on), and the placement of the mace illustrate contemporary descriptions of the appearance of the South Carolina Commons House of Assembly, which, like other colonial bodies, imitated the British example. Courtesy, Colonial Williamsburg Foundation.

offered a similar opinion, believing the "many heavy pillars & much carving, rather   **43**
superb than elegant." By contrast Webster observed that the "assembly room is of
ye same dimensions, but much plainer work. 'tis convenient enoh."[85]

There are no detailed descriptions of this simpler work found in the room of the
Commons House. The most important piece of furniture was the speaker's chair,
which commanded the center of attention. If it were similar to other ceremonial
chairs, such as the speaker's chairs in the House of Commons in London or the
much simpler one in the House of Burgesses in the capitol in Williamsburg, it would
have had a tall pedimented back, a broad seat, and arms, and would have been
raised, perhaps, on a platform a step above the surrounding floor. Replicating the
tradition of the House of Commons in London, South Carolina's speaker wore a
ceremonial wig and robe when he sat in the chair.[86] The journals of the house make
it clear that a large table was used by the clerk and others and that a bar also separated the entrance into the assembly room. What other fittings were available for the
forty or more representatives who sat in session remains uncertain. A visitor's
description of a debate in the Commons House in 1773 provides a revealing glimpse
of the rituals and deportment of the colonial legislators:

> The first thing done at the meeting of the house is to bring the mace (a very
> superb and elegant one that cost ninety guineas) and lay it on the table before
> the speaker. This I am told is the way in the Commons of G[reat] B[ritain].
>
> The next thing is for the Clerk to read over in a very audible voice, the
> doings of the preceding day.
>
> The Speaker [Rawlins Lowndes] is robed in black and has a very large wig
> of State, when he goes to attend the Chair (with the Mace borne before him)
> on delivery of speeches, etc. . . .
>
> The members of the house all sit with their hats on, and uncover when
> they rise to speak: they are not confined (at least they did not confine them-
> selves) to any one place to speak in.
>
> The members conversed, lolled, and chatted much like a friendly jovial soci-
> ety, when nothing of importance was before the house: nay once or twice while
> the speaker and clerk were busy in writing the members spoke quite loud across
> the room to one another. A very unparliamentary appearance. The speaker put
> the questions sitting, and conversed with the house sitting: the members gave
> their votes by rising from their seats, the dissentients did not rise.[87]

After the repeal of the Stamp Act in 1766, the Commons House requested that
the leading champions of its repeal and members of the Stamp Act Congress held in
New York—Thomas Lynch, Christopher Gadsden, and John Rutledge—have full-
length portraits of themselves painted and "preserved in the assembly room, as a tes-
timony of public regard." At the same time they also voted to procure a statue of
the English statesman William Pitt that would "be erected in the State House as a
memorial of their respect for him . . . particularly his assistance in procuring a repeal
of the Stamp Act." A motion was also made to erect a statue of the king as well, but

44

Engraving of John Rutledge (1739–1800). Rutledge was a South Carolina delegate to the Stamp Act Congress. Subsequently he was a member of the Continental Congress and was president and governor of South Carolina and a member of the Federal Constitutional Convention. Courtesy, South Caroliniana Library, University of South Carolina, Columbia.

it failed to be seconded by members of the assembly. A sum of £1,000 sterling was appropriated in June 1766 for the commission, and through the recommendation of Charles Garth, the provincial agent in London, the assembly selected sculptor Joseph Wilton to execute the work.[88] Garth wrote to the assembly committee that Wilton had recently finished a statue of Pitt for the town of Cork in Ireland that "was admired by every body." Some members thought the statue should be placed in the assembly room opposite the speaker's chair while others argued for an open area outside the statehouse. The sculptor seemed to favor an outdoor location where "the Statue can be disposed so as to form a *Vista* from the avenue of several large Streets," noting that "Public Monuments or Statues, erected judiciously in a City, add greatly to its Elegance and Dignity." The committee decided to have it placed just to the southeast of the statehouse in the intersection of Meeting and Broad Streets, "the most Public part of our Town."[89]

After some delay the marble statue arrived in Charleston in May 1770. Measuring seven and one-half feet in height, it depicts the statesman in a public speaking stance, holding the Magna Carta in one hand—a pose similar to the one etched by American artist Charles Willson Peale in his engraving of the great Whig leader. A brick foundation and pedestal were constructed by the Horlbeck brothers under the supervision of Wilton's assistant William Adron in the following month, and the statue was ceremoniously raised in its prominent location on the afternoon of 5 July.[90] Speaker of the House Peter Manigault climbed the scaffolding and, responding to the request of an enthusiastic crowd below, read the inscription carved on the pedestal that declared:

Statue of William Pitt, 1770, Joseph Wilton, sculptor. Installed at the intersection of Broad and Meeting Streets in July 1770, Pitt's statue was a tangible reminder of the friction that was developing between Great Britain and her American colonies in the 1760s and early 1770s. The statue remained in its original location for less than twenty-five years. After suffering some damage during the American Revolution and causing a number of traffic accidents in the early 1790s, the statue was removed to the Charleston Orphan House in 1794, and from 1881 to 1984 it stood in Washington Park, behind Charleston City Hall. Courtesy, Charleston Museum, Charleston.

In Grateful Memory of his Services to his Country in General and to America in Particular the Commons House of Assembly of South Carolina Unanimously voted this Statue of the Hon. William Pitt, Esq. Who Gloriously Exerted himself by Defending the Freedom of Americans the True Sons of England by Promoting a Repeal of the Stamp-Act in the Year 1766; Time will sooner Destroy this Mark of their Esteem than Erase from their Minds their Just Sense of his Patriotic Virtue.[91]

Following the Stamp Act, a series of imperial crises, such as the Wilkes Fund Controversy, kept the provincial government of South Carolina in constant turmoil for nearly a decade.[92] In 1775 hostilities between the Crown and colonies erupted in open conflict, followed by a declaration of independence the next year. One of the earliest acts of rebellion occurred in April 1775, when patriots broke into the armory housed in the attic of the building and seized arms and ammunition stored there. Among those responsible for this daring assault on royal authority was Edward Weyman, the upholsterer who had earlier provided the drapery for the portrait of King George in the council chamber.[93] Gradually the legally constituted authority of

46

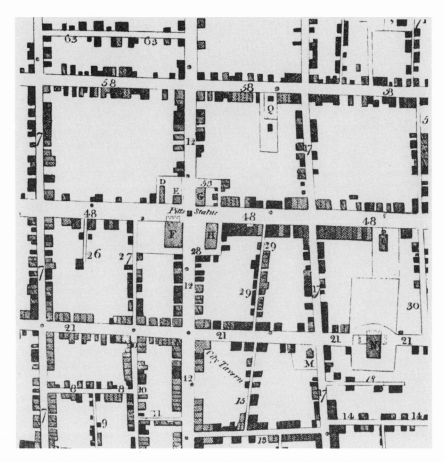

Detail of Edward Petrie's Phoenix Fire Map of 1788, showing the statehouse with its out-buildings [G] and other civic structures at the intersection of Meeting and Broad Streets, with Joseph Wilton's statue of William Pitt in the center. Courtesy, South Caroliniana Library, University of South Carolina, Columbia.

the Commons House was supplanted by a popularly elected provincial congress, many of whose members had been leaders in the royal assembly. This congress took possession of the old assembly room and began to direct the affairs of the rebellious colony.[94] The collapse of royal authority and the establishment of the state government of South Carolina had important consequences for Charleston and the statehouse. In 1780 British forces captured the city. During the two-year occupation that followed, the exigencies of war, whether deliberate acts of destruction or unintentional mishaps, caused extensive damage to many buildings, including the statehouse and the Pitt statue. In April 1780 British artillery fire managed to break off the statue's right arm, which held a copy of the Magna Carta, perhaps a symbolic severance of the ties that bound England and America to a common inheritance.[95] When the state government reoccupied Charleston following the removal of British troops, officials found that the statehouse had lost many of its furnishings.

The confusion caused by the occupation of Charleston, the uncertainty in post-war trade, and the democratic fervor unleashed by the American Revolution brought a period of unrest to Charleston in 1783 and 1784. Factious strife waged in newspaper articles erupted into riots as laborers, mechanics, and those who favored breaking the tight control of the General Assembly held by aristocratic merchants and planters vented their anger in the streets on several occasions. With feigned "reverence and respect . . . for the Assembly," these advocates of democratic reform, complained merchant Christopher Gadsden, were quick to scorn the government "not only from the Press but at the corner of almost every street." He believed that such disrespect hurt the fortunes of the city, for "what foreigners will trade with such madmen, not only regardless of, but even insulting their own Legislatures?"[96]

Perhaps, in response to these extraparliamentary assaults on their privileges and power, the General Assembly quickly moved to restore the political symbols of its authority. In 1783 the House of Representatives, which replaced the colonial Commons House, moved back into its old quarters on the second floor of the statehouse after extensive repairs were made. In order to accommodate the membership, forty-five chairs were imported from Philadelphia. The Speaker's chair in the assembly room was mended and altered. Packed as they were in a room of less than one thousand square feet, members of the lower house found themselves crowded even further by the dozens of visitors and petitioners who sought redress or entertainment from the proceedings. In 1785 carpenter Joseph Bee erected a gallery in the room "to accommodate Strangers," which must have relieved some of the backroom shuffling but surely left the space a little more claustrophobic. Elsewhere in the building, the privy council—an advisory body to the executive that was established with the 1776 constitution—moved into the Speaker's chamber in the front center of the second floor. In 1783 rooms throughout the statehouse were painted and broken windows reglazed, and in the following year a new slate roof was installed.[97] The building must have been presentable enough for renewed use by outside groups. In May 1785 it served as the venue for the first convention of the newly established Protestant Episcopal Church of South Carolina, the successor to the Church of England.[98]

Throughout the 1780s the state government continued to repair and improve the building. In order to divert a natural calamity, two new electrical conductors were installed on the roof.[99] In 1786 the House of Representatives purchased two polished pokers with brass heads to stir the fires in their chambers and covered the clerk's table with new green broadcloth.[100] Unfortunately all this work was soon lost.

THE COURTHOUSE, 1788–1883

A most perfect specimen of Palladian architecture...
Caroline Gilman, The Southern Rose, *1838*

On 5 February 1788 sparks from a fire in the senate chamber fireplace accidentally became lodged behind the wall paneling and eventually ignited a conflagration that destroyed the statehouse. The fire was discovered about nine o'clock in the evening, "but before proper assistance could be obtained, it had got to such a height as to prevent any possibility of saving that elegant building."[101] Bucket brigades formed, but this archaic and ineffective method failed to bring the fire under control although in the midst of this disaster nimble-footed volunteers managed to save most of the provincial documents lodged in the ground-floor rooms.[102] Charred

"A Scene in the Theatre—Charleston," watercolor for a set design by Charles Fraser, ca. 1792. In this view looking eastward from the intersection of Broad and Meeting Streets, one sees St. Michael's church, the Beef Market, the statehouse as rebuilt after the 1788 fire, and the statue of William Pitt in the intersection before it was removed to the Orphan House. Photograph from South Carolina Historical Society, courtesy of Caroline Winthrop Weston Cohen.

The Shire Hall, Chelmsford, Essex, England, 1789–1791, John Johnson, architect. This building, contemporary in date to the rebuilding of the statehouse, exhibits the same pattern of Palladian design as used earlier in the century for such structures but has neoclassical elements similar to the Charleston County Courthouse design. Photograph by Carl R. Lounsbury, 1990.

bond timbers and nailing blocks lodged in the brickwork on both floors of the building testify to the severity of the fire, but the brick walls were deemed strong enough to be reused during the subsequent reconstruction of the building. In an effort to provide more room in the structure, the building commissioners charged with rehabilitating the burned-out shell decided to add a third story on top of the old walls. The construction of this additional story may have been motivated by lowcountry politicians who wanted to entice the legislature back to a more commodious home in Charleston. Just prior to the fire, the legislature had voted to move the state government to a geographically more centralized area upstate and had selected Taylor's Plantation as the new capital, renaming it Columbia. Efforts to reverse this decision gradually diminished, and the old statehouse took on a new function as the Charleston County Courthouse.

Detailed accounts of the transformation of the old statehouse into the Charleston County Courthouse have disappeared. As in the case of the statehouse construction, a small building committee composed of federal, state, and county officials oversaw the rebuilding and refurbishing of the new courthouse. Although William Drayton, the first judge of the U.S. District Court for South Carolina and chairman of the commission, was suggested as the principal architect of the new work by nineteenth-century artist Charles Fraser, little is known of his or other members' part in the design process.[103] Constrained by having to use the walls of the

50   earlier structure, the building committee devised a plan that comfortably fit into late-eighteenth-century Anglo-American public building practices. The richly elaborate facade of niches, rusticated arcade, and engaged columns of the central pediment repeated a formula articulated in contemporary English public buildings such as the Shire Hall in Chelmsford, Essex (1791), and the Shire Hall in Stafford, Staffordshire (1794), and in this country was the forerunner of a similar scheme for the new President's House in Washington, D.C.[104] Besides the precedent of standing buildings, architectural publications were replete with similar forms that may have informed the deliberations of the building commissioners. James Gibbs's *Book of Architecture,* published more than sixty years prior, illustrated a number of designs with central, pedimented, engaged porticoes standing on rusticated or arcaded ground floors as well as facades punctuated by niches.[105]

The third-story addition drastically changed the structure's proportions and magnified its physical presence. To compensate for the increased height, it was necessary to widen the central pavilion by a few feet.[106] Two-story engaged Ionic columns constructed of brick with stone capitals adorned the new, three-bay pedimented projection. On the ground floor a new rusticated arcade carried the Ionic orders. The principal entrance continued to be the central door on Broad Street. However, this opening was now accentuated with the addition of Aquia sandstone quoining. The two adjoining windows retained their flat-headed openings but were, like the projecting arcade, rusticated with brick and covered with stucco.

Restored south (front) elevation of the Charleston County Courthouse as completed in 1792. Drawn by Mark R. Wenger, Colonial Williamsburg Foundation.

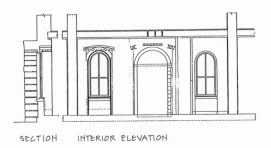

SECTION   INTERIOR ELEVATION

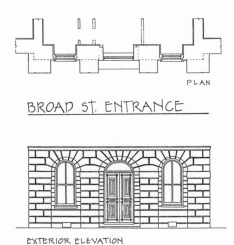

PLAN

BROAD ST. ENTRANCE

EXTERIOR ELEVATION

Plan and elevations of the Broad Street entrance to the courthouse. These detailed drawings of the central three bays of the Broad Street facade reveal that the rusticated arcade and the rustication around the front door were added following the 1788 fire. The arched window heads are also late-eighteenth-century additions. The statehouse windows first had flat heads. Measured and drawn by W. Brown Morton III, Mary Washington College, 1991.

In general the size and location of the statehouse openings did not alter dramatically during the rebuilding. However, their spacing shifted somewhat as the windows were moved eight inches outward from the central bays on the front and back walls. In the central three bays of the new front pedimented facade, the windows were not narrowed on the outside, but the interior reveals were reduced four inches on each side. Presumably this reworking of the windows responded to the widening of the central pavilion and the enlargement of the columns between the openings in this section of the facade. There is at least one significant exception. The second-floor window in the center of the east facade remains on its original center, but it was initially two feet wider than the present aperture since it served as the opening to the Meeting Street balcony during the statehouse period. Following the fire, the door was converted into a much smaller window. To compensate for this narrowing, the two adjacent windows were shifted inward toward the reduced opening. From the movement of other windows in the post-1788 rebuilding, it seems likely that the east and west facades were originally identical in the spacing of their window openings.[107] The height of the windows was reduced by about eight inches. The new sandstone lintels projected beyond the face of the surrounding stucco work and were ornamented with a large keystone. Like the lintels, the sills were fabricated

52

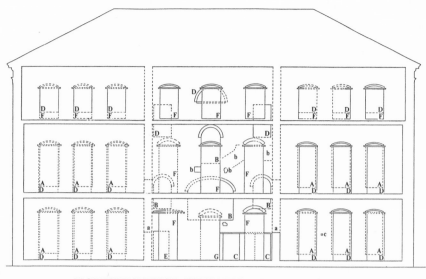

NORTH INTERIOR ELEVATION OF THE COURTHOUSE
1753-1883

A. 1753-1788 Window   a. Aperture for 1753-1788 stair
B. 1753-1883 Window   b. Evidence for 1788-1883 stair
C. 1753-1883 Door   location
D. 1788-1883 Window   c. Pocket filled 1788
E. 1788-1883 Door
F. 1883 Window
G. 1883 Door

North interior elevation of the courthouse. This drawing depicts the position and alterations of apertures on the rear or north wall of the courthouse from 1753 to 1883. Following the statehouse fire in 1788, the windows on the two original lower floors were shifted a few inches from their previous position. Major alterations were made to the apertures in 1883. The most disruptive were the removal of the main staircase in the central three bays and the lowering of the third-story windows. Drawing by Mark R. Wenger, Colonial Williamsburg Foundation, 1991.

of imported sandstone. Many of the ground-floor and second-story apertures on the east and south facades retain their 1790s window frames although the decorative architrave moldings and sash were replaced in subsequent renovations.[108]

Both the east and west exterior doors were rebuilt at this time. In both cases the openings were narrowed, and below the square head new masonry infill corbelled out to create a circular-headed opening on the interior while a semicircular brick arch carried the masonry on the exterior. To accentuate the openings, sandstone quoins were added below the arch, and a formal frontispiece with engaged columns supporting a pedimented Ionic entablature framed the opening. Much, if not all, of these two frontispieces was fabricated, like the window lintels and sills, from the increasingly popular Aquia sandstone, quarried in Stafford County, Virginia. In the same decade, for example, stone masons in Washington, D.C., employed this easily worked, buff-colored stone for the trim in a number of public buildings, including the White House and Capitol.

The courthouse sandstone arrived in Charleston from Virginia aboard the schooner *Betsey* in September 1788. The commissioners hired Robert Given, a stone-cutter who had settled in Charleston in the mid-1780s, to fabricate the window lintels, sills, east and west frontispieces, and the door surrounds, cornice, and Ionic capitals of the south facade. A few years later, when Given was seeking employment on the federal buildings in the District of Columbia, William Moultrie recommended him to George Washington as "an industrious sober man" whose stonework on the courthouse was done "in a masterly manner.[109]

The courthouse building commissioners made a number of other significant changes to the exterior. Niches in the second and eighth bays replaced window openings on the two lower floors, echoing hemispherical recesses in the new walls of the third story.[110] Molded string courses now articulated the division between the second and third floors. Further ornamentation in the form of quoins was added at the corners of the building and the central pavilion, perhaps replacing earlier work of a similar nature. The entire building was crowned by a low-hipped roof with four chimney stacks projecting high above the roofline. Whether immediately upon rebuilding or at some unknown date afterward, two widely spaced dormers were constructed on the north slope of the roof. Even though the building was re-stuccoed shortly after the fire, the entire exterior was given a new coat of rough casting "in imitation of Stone" by plasterer Thomas Duggan in 1825.[111] Ten years later the building was finished "in imitation of granite," which, according to one newspaper account, "reflects no little credit on the judgment and taste of the plan, as also on the skill and fidelity of the architect who executed it." Gone were the "dull and uninteresting" colors of the previous period in favor of a "manner well calculated to display those classical proportions and ornaments, which are the result of a correct system of architecture. The chaste columns of the Ionic order, on the Southern front, shining with the reflected lustre of the noon day sun, or brightened by the silver radiance of the moon, cannot fail to please all who contrast them with their former dark and discolored character."[112]

Although rebuilding the ruined shell began immediately after the fire, the commissioners for the courthouse soon ran into the same financial problems that beset their predecessors on the statehouse.[113] The completion of the building was a long, drawn-out affair, with ground-floor chambers remaining unfinished for nearly twenty years. Although the federal courtroom on the second floor was far enough along for U.S. Supreme Court associate justice Thomas Johnson and South Carolina District judge Thomas Bee to convene the federal circuit court there in October 1792, the bare brick walls in other parts of the building testified to the slowness of the work.[114] A presentment brought by a grand jury in September 1796 called for the South Carolina legislature to "make ample provision for finishing so Elegant and useful a Building."[115] Despite the grand jury's request, little was done to complete the interior for more than a decade. A visitor in 1805 described the building as "outwardly, very decent; but, inwardly rather coarse."[116] If work was slow, payment lagged even further behind schedule. A veteran of many public and private building

54   projects in the city, bricklayer Anthony Toomer spent nearly nine years repairing the old walls and completing the new third floor, yet several years after he had died, his widow petitioned the legislature to pay the balance still due the estate.[117]

As late as 1808 much of the interior still remained unfinished. In September of that year the commissioners advertised for bricklayers to lath and plaster parts of the inside and roughcast the exterior. They needed carpenters to repair the stairs, make new sash windows, and fabricate fasteners for the shutters. Painters were needed to finish various parts of the building as well as repair and paint the tin pipes and gutters and the stone cornice of the pedimented south front.[118] Despite this appeal, few craftsmen jumped at the opportunity, perhaps afraid that they would end up like Toomer with little to show for their labor. The next year a detailed list was made of work still needing attention. The entry hall and the passage in the eastern section of the ground floor required plastering.[119] The register of mesne conveyance office on the second floor also lacked plastering, while the prothonotary's office in the southeast room on the ground floor needed whitewashing. This latter room still had no shelves for papers or books, and most other offices lacked tables and chairs.[120] It is readily evident from the surviving trim of the door jambs leading into the west ground-floor courtroom and the east corridor that this work was not executed until the end of the decade or in the 1810s. Fashionable quirk moldings and the use of technologically advanced machine-manufactured brads attest to the long period of refurbishing. The few fragments that have survived from this rebuilding reveal that the character of the woodwork was probably of a lighter, neoclassical detailing rather than the heavier forms of a quarter century earlier. Craftsmen eventually performed the many tasks laid out by the commissioners, and the courthouse assumed the form and finish it would retain until the radical changes of the 1880s.[121] By the time of his survey of Charleston in 1826, architect Robert Mills could declare without exaggeration that the courthouse "is another of those substantial and well arranged buildings which do credit to the art."[122] A dozen years later another critic effusively described it as "a most perfect specimen of Palladian architecture."[123]

GROUND-FLOOR PLAN

The functions of the courthouse varied significantly from those of the colonial statehouse, and the commissioners charged with rebuilding the structure changed the stair circulation to reflect those differences. The primary entrance from Broad Street still led into a large lobby with a grand stair ascending to the main courtrooms on the second floor. Like the original, this stairway rose along the central axis at the back of the lobby and, after reaching the first landing below the Venetian window, split and ascended in two separate flights along the north wall. But the openings through the transverse walls were now blocked, and the upper flights of the stair turned back on itself and rose along both these walls to a common landing on the second floor. This alteration probably used the central circulation space more efficiently and freed up a substantial portion of the second floor.

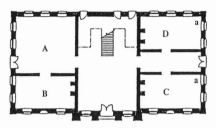

FIRST FLOOR PLAN

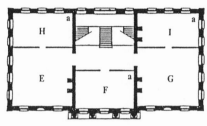

SECOND FLOOR PLAN

A. Court of Sessions &
      Common Pleas
B. Judges' Chambers
C. Prothonotary's Office
D. Sheriff's Office
E. Court of Equity
F. Register of Mesne
      Conveyance until 1826;
      S.C. Law Society
      Library, 1826
G. U.S. District Court
H. Register of the Court
      of Equity
I. Clerk of U.S. District
      Court & U.S. Marshal
J. Jury Rooms
K. State Treasurer until
      1826; Jury Room; &
      Medical Society until
      mid 1820s
L. State Comptroller
      & Grand Jury
M. Charleston Library
      Society & Museum
      until the 1820s

a. Subdivision of space
      unknown

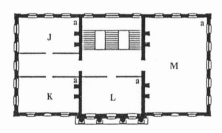

THIRD FLOOR PLAN

Conjectural plan of the Charleston courthouse, 1792–1883. Measured by Mark R. Wenger, Carl R. Lounsbury, and Willie Graham. Drawing by Willie Graham, Colonial Williamsburg Foundation.

To reach the third-floor jury rooms and the space occupied by the Charleston Library Society, the stair repeated the same pattern. The slope of this stair can be traced by marks it left on the brickwork on the north wall and east partition. The uppermost landings to the third floor were lit by small, square, flat-headed openings while the landing between the second and third floor retained the original opening with the top rebuilt to form a compass-headed window. At the top of the third floor, a larger lunette or D-shaped window crowned the center of this well-lit stairwell. On the outside the central section of this north wall looked like the backside of many

56   Charleston residences where apertures of many shapes and sizes pierced the brickwork in a variety of patterns. The various positions of the arched, segmental, and
square-headed windows that were crowded into this section provided a sharp contrast to the regularity of the openings found elsewhere in the building.

The major brick partitions, which separated the building into thirds, continued
to influence the layout and use of the new courthouse. The large room in the western section of the ground floor, used as a courtroom during the colonial period, continued in that capacity and retained the same means of access as the earlier one.
Through the first decades of the new century, the Courts of Common Pleas and General Sessions met here.[124] The central door on the west facade opened into the lower
end of the courtroom or west passage and was again probably balanced by another
door opening opposite it from the lobby. One slight modification to the colonial
arrangement occurred with the creation of a door in place of the westernmost window in the north wall at some later date in the nineteenth century. Perhaps this door
provided direct access into the courtroom for magistrates or possibly for prisoners
led in from a holding room in the jailer's house in the rear courtyard. This arrangement reflected a growing tendency across America in the early nineteenth century to
segregate various court participants through a series of private chambers, separate
corridors, and segregated entrances. These new circulation patterns allowed judges
to escape the taunts of an angry crowd, prevented spectators from harassing or
influencing jurors, and provided a measure of security in transporting criminals to
the dock.

An extract from the rules of court published in 1806 provides a glimpse of how
the space within the lawyers' bar was divided. One of these rules noted "that the
inner bench of the court be reserved for the elder practitioners of the bar, the second
bench to be occupied by the younger practitioners, and the outer bench by the stu-
dents at law. The gentlemen of the bar to take their seats according to seniority of
the dates of their respective admissions." Compared to the near chaotic decorum
found in a number of courtrooms across the country, the Charleston legal fraternity
clearly preferred to rely upon orderly precedent in their suits and seats.[125] Just
behind the bar a door opened into the southwest chamber, which functioned as the
judge's chambers. This was the only access to this space through the antebellum
period.[126]

In the eastern section of the courthouse, the lateral corridor remained with one
door opening off the entry hall and the other opening in the center of the east facade
on Meeting Street. In the first decades of the nineteenth century, the southeast room
was the office of the prothonotary, who served as the clerk of the Courts of Common Pleas and General Sessions. The original doorway into this office was narrowed
slightly by filling in the east jamb about twelve inches. Opposite this space in the
northeast room was the sheriff's office. Here too the earlier doorway to the corridor
was narrowed slightly. Traces of plaster from the late eighteenth or early nineteenth
century imply that this room was plastered from floor to ceiling, having no cornice
or chair board. Paint analysis of surviving plaster fragments indicates that the walls

of this office were first painted a reddish brown.[127] A doorway was cut in through   *57*
the easternmost window in the north or rear wall to allow the sheriff to come and
go directly into the back courtyard. This doorway received an Aquia sandstone sill,
which managed to survive a number of later alterations.

SECOND-FLOOR PLAN

As in the statehouse period, the second floor contained the two principal rooms.
Because the transverse walls continued to divide the building into thirds, the size of
the upper rooms probably matched those of the statehouse era. The two principal
courts occupied the large rooms in the southeast and southwest corners, where the
colonial council and Commons House had once assembled. The Court of Equity
convened in the west end of the building while the circuit and U.S. District Court
met in the east room—a spatial arrangement perhaps reflecting the earlier cachet
associated with the room of the upper house.[128] Federal judge Thomas Bee first
opened court in this room on 11 December 1792, and it was to remain the home of
the U.S. District Court until 1837, when it moved to new quarters in the Planter's
Hotel one block to the north. In the Jacksonian era the courtroom provided a forum
for debate over the nature of state and federal authority in cases involving slavery
and tariffs, which culminated in the early 1830s in the nullification crisis. In 1828
Congress passed a tariff designed mainly to protect American industries against for-
eign competition but placed a high duty on cotton, woolens, and iron. In the Bond
case argued in September 1831 in the district court, Judge Thomas Lee actively supported the authority of the United States government against those who argued in
favor of the state's right to nullify the federal tariff on cotton, which many South
Carolina planters found particularly odious.[129] Such a unionist stronghold in the
midst of impassioned nullifiers probably galled the latter and in part may have been
an underlying factor in the removal of the federal presence from the county courthouse half a dozen years later.

In calmer times long before the nullification crisis, the courtroom saw the peri-
odic appearance of members of the U.S. Supreme Court who traveled the southern
circuit to interpret the laws of the new federal constitution.[130] Associate justices such
as James Iredell, Thomas Johnson, Alfred Moore, Bushrod Washington, James Wil-
son, and William Cushing, and chief justices Oliver Ellsworth of Connecticut and
his predecessor, South Carolina native John Rutledge, undertook extensive journeys
each fall in order to hear cases with district judges in federal courtrooms in Richmond, Raleigh, and other cities before making their way to Charleston. Their
appearance in town received considerable notice, and much of their time outside the
courtroom was occupied in conversing and dining with local officials, lawyers, and
other leading political figures. Absences, delays, and illnesses often prevented the
prompt convening of the federal courts, forcing justices to extend their stays in the
city. On one such occasion Justice Iredell took advantage of the extra time to tour
the city and attend a dance.[131] The solemn ceremonies that marked the opening of
the federal court must have been particularly satisfying to many South Carolinians

58   when, in October 1795, Chief Justice Rutledge took his place on the bench along-
side district judge Bee in the U.S. Circuit Courtroom.[132] Unaware of the circuit riding of the Supreme Court justices, a visitor to the U.S. District Court in the 1820s
observed that "for the first time in an American Court, except the Supreme at Washington, I saw the judge in legal costume. He was arrayed in a black cloak with
Geneva bands hanging from his neckcloth."[133] The visitor may well have seen one of
the U.S. Supreme Court justices or perhaps the resident federal magistrate.

The register of the Court of Equity had an office in the back western section,
but how it communicated with the courtroom and the stair hall remains uncertain.
Presumably entrance into this rear office was through the courtroom. A bar at the
north end of the courtroom would have placed the door to the offices within the
public space at the back of the room, making access to the office less disruptive during court sessions. The office of the federal clerk and U.S. marshal in the northeast
section probably had the same arrangement. Evidence in both the east and west
front rooms suggests that these courtrooms were plastered from floor to ceiling during the early years.

The federal courtroom was decorated in a modest but up-to-date fashion. During the earliest years the walls were painted yellow.[134] A twelve-inch cornice crowned
the federal courtroom, which measured sixteen feet, ten inches from floor to ceiling.
Part of a decorative cornice frieze with regularly spaced gouges of abstracted Doric
triglyphs was discovered in 1991 being used as a nailer for the west door surround
on the ground floor. Although its original location is uncertain, the fragment provides a tantalizing glimpse of the form and quality of the early-nineteenth-century
woodwork that once ornamented the courtroom and other parts of the building.
The gouged cornice and the quirk moldings of the west ground-floor doorway suggest that the courthouse was trimmed with the same neoclassical motifs found in
other public and domestic structures erected in Charleston between 1805 and 1825.
The drawing room of the Heyward House at 31 Legare Street, for example, has a
similar gouged cornice frieze.[135] Other now-lost elements of the courthouse woodwork may have been comparable to the earliest woodwork surviving in the neighboring Hebrew Orphanage on Broad Street, which was constructed in the first years
of the new century.

In the center section of the building at the head of the stair landing was the
office of the register of mesne conveyance and the clerk of the Court of Equity.[136] Two
mortises in the top of the south girder spanning the first-floor entry hall provide evidence for the location of a doorway into this office. Embracing the three bays of the
central pavilion, this office also was originally plastered from floor to ceiling. Physical evidence for the subdivision of this space, if it were partitioned into rooms for
the register and clerk, is not evident. Surviving floor framing indicates that this space
was heated, perhaps, like its colonial predecessor, by two fireplaces centered on the
east and west partition walls. After the Fireproof Building was constructed in 1826
just north of the courthouse on the corner of Meeting and Chalmers Streets, the register of mesne conveyance and state offices such as the treasurer and comptroller

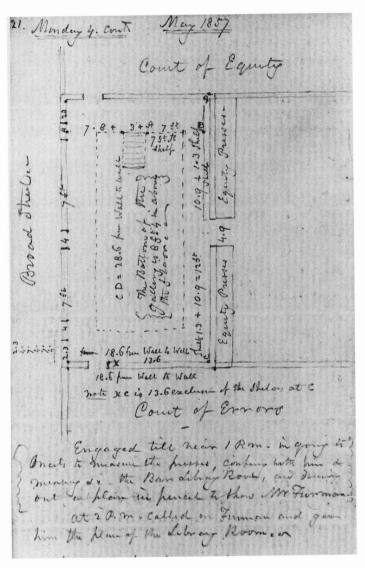

Plan of second-story library, Charles Parker Notebook, no. 143, Charles Parker Papers, South Carolina Historical Society. Courtesy, South Carolina Historical Society, Charleston.

moved to these new quarters. Following removal of the register of mesne conveyance, the library of the South Carolina Bar Association occupied this room.[137] By the late 1850s the space was filled with shelves and book presses and subdivided into two levels. A narrow gallery encircled the entire room eight and one-half feet above the floor and was reached by a ladder at the west end. Doorways led from the law library into the Court of Equity on the west and to the appellate Court for the Correction of Errors in the east in the room where the federal court had once convened.[138]

60   THIRD-FLOOR PLAN

The addition of the third floor provided space for a variety of offices and functions. Investigation of the surviving fabric of the building confirms the former existence of brick transverse walls separating the third floor—like the two below it—into three nearly equal sections. One or more jury rooms, which served the three courtrooms, were located in the west and central section of the third floor.[139] In the northwest corner of the building, a series of wooden nailers within the brickwork suggest that the room was originally finished with a chair board. The rooms listed in Charleston directories of the first decades of the nineteenth century noted that the office of the state treasurer occupied the southwest corner of the building and that the comptroller's office was in the south central section although the exact size of these spaces remains uncertain. The southwest corner of the building must have been subdivided into at least two rooms since one part of it was used as a jury room. By 1806 the Medical Society of South Carolina was holding its monthly meetings here and had fitted it out with bookcases filled with its collection of medical texts and items of related interest.[140] At these monthly meetings the leading physicians in the city, often accompanied by visiting colleagues, discussed the causes of diseases such as yellow fever and debated ways to remedy the outbreak of epidemics, such as by providing better sanitation for the city's inhabitants. They continued to occupy this space in the courthouse until the medical college was chartered and opened in separate quarters in the mid-1820s.[141]

The most popular part of the third floor was the eastern section, which embraced several rooms housing the Charleston Library Society and a small museum of natural history. The Library Society had subscribed money for rebuilding the statehouse after it had burned and was rewarded with space on the third floor to house its collection of books. The society had been established by a group of Charleston merchants and other inhabitants in 1748 as a circulating library, which grew into a sizable collection by the time it moved into the courthouse in 1790.[142] The Charleston Museum, established in 1773, soon followed the Library Society as a tenant on the third floor. Many private donations of birds, insects, minerals, and other curiosities over the next quarter century significantly increased its collections. By 1807 Mr. Gagne, the proprietor of the museum, prevailed upon the Medical Society to allow him to display many of his specimens in their room next to the Library Society. At that time the museum opened its doors every day of the week except Sundays and charged an admission price of fifty cents for adults and twenty-five cents for children.[143]

Nearly every visitor to the city in the first two decades of the nineteenth century climbed the grand stair to the third floor to view the city's cultural showplace. As with many other early museums and libraries in America, these rooms offered a cabinet of curiosities where the exotic and esoteric provided entertainment and edification. Birds, mammals, minerals, fossils, and shells collected from Europe, Africa, and the Americas vied for visitors' attention along with unusual cultural artifacts such as a native grass helmet from the Sandwich Islands (Hawaii), a pair of Chinese

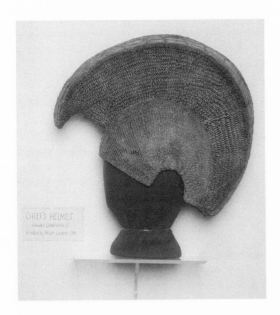

Grass helmet from the Sandwich Islands, late eighteenth century. This helmet, made for a Hawaiian chieftain, was presented to the Charleston Museum in 1798. It is the only object still in the museum's collection that was originally housed in the courthouse. Courtesy, Charleston Museum, Charleston.

chopsticks, and ancient Indian tools from a burying ground at nearby Goose Creek.[144] Among the more curious specimens advertised in this collection of nearly six hundred species was "L'Homme de Bois or a kind of Ourang-outang."[145] Another popular exhibit was two poorly preserved Egyptian mummies with "black and smelly" skin with the texture of a "dry leaf only harder."[146] Most admired what they saw, describing the library as well stocked with modern works and nicely decorated with large prints depicting scenes from Shakespeare's plays. English traveler John Lambert provided one of the most detailed descriptions of this period. He observed that although:

> the lower parts of the building are much out of repair . . . the upper apartments are kept in good order. . . . The library contains about 4,000 volumes, well selected and arranged. . . . The library contains Boydell's elegant edition of Shakespeare, and the large prints are framed, and hung round the room. The portraits of the king and queen belonging to that edition are placed on either side the door-way leading to the inner room. . . . There is a large painting, executed by a Mr. White, of Charleston, exhibited in the library, and is considered a very favourable effort for a young artist. The subject is the murder of Prince Arthur . . . some new casts from the Apollo, Belvidere, Venus de Medicis, Venus rising from the sea &c. were deposited in the library to be exhibited for a short time. They were the property of Mr. Middleton and had lately arrived from Paris. The library also contains a few natural curiosities, such as fossils, minerals, mammoth bones, snakes, armadilloes, poisonous insects in spirits &c. and two remarkable deer's horn which were found locked in each other. . . . A Museum has been lately established by a gentleman who occupies a room adjoining the library. His collection at present contains chiefly birds.[147]

A scene from Shakespeare's *Merry Wives of Windsor*, act 2, scene 1, painted by William Peters, engraved by Robert Thew, 1793, published by John Boydell and Josiah Boydell, London. Prints from this edition lined the third-floor room of the Charleston Library Society. Courtesy, Colonial Williamsburg Foundation.

How this section of the building occupied by the Library Society was arranged is uncertain. A visitor in 1817 observed that "the room is divided into five or six apartments not in the manner of alcoves like Harvard and Yale libraries, but by ceilings which have openings little wider than are required for doors."[148] Evidence of this division remains obscure. This may be due in part to the fact that the plaster finish was not applied directly to the face of the brick but attached to riven lath nailed into wooden furring strips. These continuous strips, running from floor to ceiling, indicate that, unlike the northwest room, no chair board was provided. Whatever its arrangement, visitors such as J. P. Dunlop concurred that the library was "an agreeable place to spend a forenoon." For those who wished to read or study the

The original statehouse columns partially survived the reconstruction of the early 1790s, embedded beneath the brickwork of the central arcaded pavilion of the courthouse. This view shows the westernmost stuccoed column at ground-floor level, exposed during the renovations of the courthouse in 2000. Analysis of the 3/16-inch-thick stucco, which covered the brick columns from at least 1768 until the fire twenty years later, revealed that the columns were not painted during this time. See page 26 for an elevation drawing and description of these columns. Photograph by Jim Wigley, 2000.

curiosities and specimens, the rooms were provided with seats and desks.[149] With its growing collections, the museum vacated the third-floor rooms in the early 1820s.[150] However, the Library Society remained in the courthouse until it purchased and moved into the South Carolina Bank building at the corner of Church and Broad Streets in 1835. Before it left its residence of forty-five years, the society boasted a collection of more than eighteen thousand books, "among which are works of great cost, and high, literary, and scientific value—as the work on Egypt prepared under the auspices of Bonaparte, in 11 imperial volumes of plates, and 25 octavo volumes of explanations and memoires; Audubon's Ornithology, expense, $800—two copies of English Encyclopëdia of different dates—800 sets of Novels—Standard French works, among which are the Dictionnaire Raisonné des Sciences &c.—29 vols valuable Engravings—the Shakespeare Gallery, consisting of 92 prints in gilt frames."[151]

MODERNIZATION
OF THE COURTHOUSE,
1883

Antebellum Agitation for Change

The commitment made in 1788 to reuse the brick partition walls of the statehouse limited the ability of the courthouse commissioners to design spaces that would entirely match the needs of the new tenants, a problem that would plague public officials for the next two centuries. The large amount of space given over to circulation in the center of the building suited the ceremonial requirements of a provincial statehouse but took up too much space in a working courthouse that required additional smaller, heated rooms for clerks, judges, juries, and other court officials. In the first forty years in which this building served as the federal and state courthouse, there was no discernible problem with the arrangement of the three courts and their ancillary offices.

However, by the middle of the nineteenth century, the growth of the city and region spawned an increasing workload, and the courts began to feel confined by the spatial arrangement provided for them in the 1790s. The removal of several state offices to Robert Mills's Fireproof Building in the 1820s and the transfer of the U.S. District Court to the Planter's Hotel in 1837 finally leveled the status and function of the building to that of other South Carolina county courthouses but provided more space for the remaining state and local courts and offices. Yet, because the brick partition walls divided the building into three equal sections, these vacated rooms could not be consolidated into larger, more spacious courtrooms unless the building was radically altered. Courtrooms no more than thirty by thirty feet could scarcely accommodate the increasing caseloads, more lawyers, and appropriate seating for court officials and the public. Their size was smaller than most found in rural county courthouses, especially the ones erected throughout the state in the 1820s by Robert Mills that contained courtrooms with nearly twice the square footage.[152]

In the fall of 1854 a grand jury clearly voiced the opinion of those who worked in the courthouse: "Having examined and to some extent experienced the inconvenience and unsuitableness of our Court House to the proper accommodations and comfort of those charged with administering the laws, the Jury recommends that extensive alterations and additions be made to the present building with as little delay as possible."[153] Although it advocated that money be set aside in the General

Assembly for improvements to the building, nothing was immediately done. In 1856   65
another grand jury reiterated the belief that the courthouse was "wholly inadequate
for the business of the Court and its Officers," being entirely "too small and uncom-
fortable." The grand jury suggested that the "Court House be so enlarged and
improved as to afford a large and more commodious Court Room below [on the
ground floor], commodious offices for the Clerk and Sheriff, and improved and
enlarged Court Room and offices in the second story, improved Jury Rooms, furnished with chimneys, or some means by which Juries may be kept comfortable in
the winter season." Outraged by the deficiency of these rooms to the "comfort of
citizens, who, in the discharge of a sacred duty, are often detained for hours in their
seats," it recommended that "under the advisement of a competent architect, the
building might be sufficiently improved to meet the exigency by an addition to the
back, or by the erection of a wing or wings of corresponding architecture."[154]
Despite the grand jury's admonition, nothing came of the proposed expansion.
Insufficient money was appropriated by the General Assembly to commission the
construction of the much-needed wing. Only some minor cosmetic improvements
were made to the interior furnishings.[155]

    Efforts to alleviate the inadequacies of the courthouse seemed on the verge of
fruition when, in October 1860, the *Charleston Mercury* announced that "plans for
improving the Court House have been completed and decided upon and that the

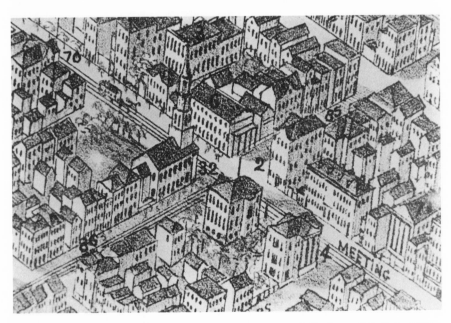

Detail showing Charleston courthouse [2], "Birds Eye View of Charleston," C. Drie, 1872.
In this detail, the multiple windows of the rear elevation are apparent. The central section of
the back wall is where the 1860 addition would have appeared had it been built. Courtesy,
South Carolina Historical Society, Charleston.

66 estimates are called for by the 1st of the ensuing month."[156] These plans called for
the demolition of the keeper's house and privies behind the building and the construction of a three-story fireproof wing. This new addition was to be sixty-two feet
wide and built against the center five bays of the north wall, extending northward
fifty feet to the back alley. The central feature was a grand, two-story, forty-nine-by-
fifty-eight-foot courtroom, with fireproof offices below lining a central corridor running north to south. The staircase in the central lobby of the old section was to be
rebuilt so that two flights of steps would rise from the ground-floor entrance rather
than one central run of stairs. After turning at a landing, the stairs would lead into
the new Courts of Common Pleas and General Sessions on the second floor. Private
stairs, chambers, and jury rooms at the north end of the new addition would provide judges, jurors, and members of the bar with discrete access into the courtroom.
A bar running through the center of the courtroom would segregate court officials
from the 250 seats provided for spectators. Puffed up to a Charleston scale, the
arrangement of the proposed addition, containing fireproof offices on either side of
a ground-floor corridor with a large courtroom and jury chambers above, followed
a pattern developed by architect Robert Mills in his designs for South Carolina
county courthouses in the 1820s that had become standardized throughout much of
the South by the middle of the century.[157]

Despite the drastic change envisioned with this massive addition, the newspaper reassured readers that the "commissioners have shown great and becoming
respect for the architectural design of the old building." Except for the change to the
stairs, "all the interior arrangements of the present building will be preserved." Fore-
shadowing a similar design solution some eighty years later, the elevation of the new
addition was to match "the old building in every particular."[158] Two months to the
day after the announced plans of expansion, delegates from across the state convened at the South Carolina Institute Hall just north of the courthouse on Meeting
Street to formally sign an Ordinance of Secession from the Union. Plans for expanding the courthouse were shelved as South Carolinians turned their attention to war.

DESIGN CONFLICT

Ceremony versus Office Space

The Civil War put an end to any hope of undertaking major changes to the courthouse. As in the American Revolution, the building escaped a major catastrophe but
suffered minor damage from shelling and four years of neglect. In an effort to restore
"the ancient and accustomed tribunals of justice," the Courts of Common Pleas and
General Sessions met in January 1866 for the first time since the cessation of hostilities but were hampered by "the deranged condition of the various offices." During
the war many of the records and court papers had been removed to the Yorkville
district further upcountry for safekeeping.[159] As Charlestonians grappled with the
economic and social dislocation wrought by the war, the courthouse lost the remaining luster it may have had as one of the central adornments of the city. Few public
ceremonies were held at the courthouse in the postbellum period. For example,

View of the courthouse following the Civil War, before alterations transformed its appearance and orientation. C. Drie, 1872. Courtesy, Historic Charleston Foundation.

when Confederate Gen. James Connor died in 1883, his body lay in state in the recently refurbished council chamber of the City Hall across the street.[160] Any civic pride that the courthouse may have evoked nearly disappeared as the building became the place where the miseries and malfeasance of the seamier side of Charleston life were brought to public attention before the local tribunals. Occasionally a sensational murder trial brought people flocking to the cramped courtroom on the second floor, but for the most part the docket consisted of a steady stream of petty larcenies, assaults, prostitution, perjuries, and burglaries. Ringing this magnet of misfortune along Courthouse Square and Broad Street were the offices of Charleston's legal profession, whose occupants routinely pleaded the cases of miscreants and malefactors.

Nearly two decades after the war, Charleston's improving fortunes and the end of Reconstruction provided an opportunity to thoroughly renovate the building to suit the needs of an overburdened judicial system. On the eve of those improvements, Arthur Mazyck observed in his descriptive overview of the city that "though this building is one of the finest ornaments of the city, its interior arrangements are not correspondingly handsome or convenient. Too much space is lost in the halls and corridors, and the court-room is not large enough for the increased business of Charleston." Yet he noted that "these major defects will probably be remedied in

68   the next few years. Attention has already been directed to the subject of remodeling the building, and there is reason to hope that Charleston will before long have a court-house as well fitted within as it is handsomely outwardly."[161] In June 1883 the Charleston County commissioners approved the plans and specifications for a major renovation of the building devised by the local architects and civil engineers John K. Gourdin and Frederick J. Smith. The adopted plan called for "the removal of the entire first two floors of the Courthouse building. The second floor will be converted into a large and airy [court]room, with private rooms for the judge, solicitor, &c. On the first floor will be located the offices of the sheriff, clerk of court, master and judicial trial justices. On the third floor will be located the jury rooms."[162] Although the long-standing desire to correct the defects of the earlier plan was about to come to pass, it was not to universal applause. One sage critic warned that "whoever shall undertake to 'improve' its architecture will do no good to the building and as little to himself."[163]

THE NEW PLAN

In late July the county commissioners awarded the contract for remodeling the courthouse to the lowest bidder, two Charleston builders of long experience, John E. Kerregan and C. McK. Grant. Kerregan had worked on the Wagener Building on East Bay Street in 1880 and had executed the carpentry at the Charleston Cotton Factory while Grant's major projects included the Crafts School and finishing the Agricultural Hall. Their bid for all work on the courthouse, excluding the new heating system, amounted to $14,785.[164] When these contractors had completed their task in late January 1884, the building was thoroughly transformed inside and out. As in 1860, the driving force was not the turn of Victorian architectural aesthetics against the rather severe neoclassical exterior but the need to provide a satisfactory and efficient courtroom space. Rather than following the antebellum plan that called for a large courtroom wing on the north side, the county commissioners radically altered the generous interior circulation pattern by destroying the transverse walls that had divided the two upper floors into thirds. By removing these brick partitions, they created a second-floor courtroom that was larger than the restrictive thirty-foot wide spaces that had been dictated by their presence. In order to accomplish this, Kerregan and Grant supported the third floor with steel tension rods suspended from a set of roof trusses aligned with new wooden partition walls on the third floor. With the removal of these walls and the installation of a modern heating system, the four late-eighteenth-century chimney stacks were removed and the slate roof patched where they had pierced the roof.

The construction of the expanded second-floor courtroom required a radical reorientation of the building's circulation pattern by ninety degrees. Deploring the wasteful inefficiency of "the large lobby on the first floor, which formerly served as a famous lounging place for idlers," the commissioners sought to make better use of this space. The contractors swept away the grand central stairway, flooring it over and replacing it with a double stair at the east end of the building. In order to

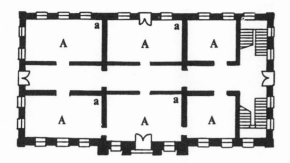

FIRST FLOOR PLAN

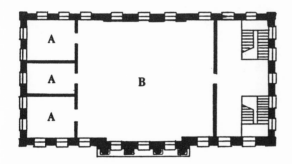

SECOND FLOOR PLAN

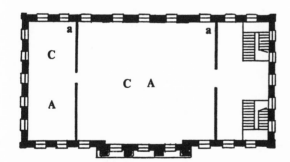

THIRD FLOOR PLAN

A. Office
B. Courtroom
C. Jury room

a. Subdivision of space unknown

Conjectural plan of the courthouse, 1883–1926. Measured by Mark R. Wenger, Carl R. Lounsbury, and Willie Graham. Drawing by Willie Graham, Colonial Williamsburg Foundation.

The cut bricks indicate the location of one of the former transverse walls. Photograph by Willie Graham, Colonial Williamsburg Foundation, 1991.

accentuate this new entry and circulation space, they removed the earlier arched and quoined doorway on the Meeting Street facade and replaced it with a sizable, pedimented, granite doorway of classical design fabricated by Edward T. Viett, a European émigré who had come to Charleston in the 1870s to carve the capitals and other decorative marble work at the Custom House. In the tympanum of the broken arch pediment stood the figure of Justice, "holding in one hand a drawn sword, and in the other the symbolic scales."[165]

The removal of the central stair and ground-floor courtroom in the western section provided the remodelers with the opportunity to construct offices for the sheriff, clerk of the courts, and masters of equity out of these spaces. A corridor wall was constructed on the north side of the west door to match the original one on the eastern section of the building. The area where the original stair was located was also partitioned in line with this north longitudinal corridor wall to form additional offices. However, access through the building from the now demoted Broad Street entrance was retained. A door on the north wall in the center of the building was created to provide access to the two remaining outbuildings in the rear courtyard, replacing the earlier doors to the rear yard. Secondary doors were also cut into the southeast and southwest rooms through the original transverse walls near their junction with the front wall. The long narrow corridor that ran from the Courthouse

View of the roof of the courthouse from the steeple of St. Michael's Episcopal Church before the 1883 renovations. Courtesy, Historic Charleston Foundation.

View of the courthouse from St. Michael's Church after the renovations of 1883 but before the 1886 earthquake. Patches in the slate roof reveal the former location of the eighteenth-century chimney stacks. By 1886 the slate roof had been replaced with a metal one. Courtesy, Historic Charleston Foundation.

72   Square entrance on the west to the stairs at the east end of the building on Meeting Street was paved with blue and white tiles and lit by three chandeliers.[166]

The new double stairway led to the new courtroom, which occupied nearly half of the second floor. At the top of the stair was a large entrance vestibule with a room off each side. One of the anterooms provided a place for witnesses to wait before their appearance in the courtroom. The other served as a temporary holding room for prisoners brought before the bar. Court officials and the public entered into the grand second-floor courtroom through large sliding doors, over which was a ground-glass transom. Covering the floor was a white cocoa matting. A newspaper account described the courtroom fittings soon after the remodeling:

> The judge's seat is on a raised platform at the west end of the room, and on each side of the judge's seat are desks for the sheriff and the stenographer. The room is divided into three parts. The western division will be occupied by the officers of the court, the central division will be devoted to the use of the bar, and the eastern division will be set apart for the public. The ceilings, which are high and airy, are surrounded by wooden cornices, and the side walls are relieved by fluted wooden pilasters. There are three chandeliers suspended from the ceiling and bracket lights on the side walls, making in all thirty-eight gas jets in the room. At the back of the judge's desk is an arched doorway through which entrance is gained to the judge's private room. In the space over the door is a palmetto tree with the coat of arms of the State at the base.
>
> The courtroom is connected by speaking tubes with the down-stairs offices, and promises to be, in every respect, adapted to the purpose for which it is intended. . . . The courtroom is painted in two shades of drab, the railings dividing the room being of black walnut, and the ceilings and side walls being left white. The acoustic properties of the room are excellent, and a person speaking in a low tone voice at one end of the room can be distinctly heard at the other end. This will be a great comfort to the members of the bar and the officers of the court. . . . The jurors will sit on raised platforms on the north and south sides of the room, and the witnesses will occupy stands on either side of the judge's stand.[167]

The new courtroom certainly met the approbation of those who began using the refurbished building during the February 1884 term of the Court of General Sessions. The presiding magistrate, Judge Joseph B. Kershaw, praised the county commissioners for furnishing the county at last "with a Courtroom and Courthouse building the appointments of which are such as become the city of Charleston, the chief city of the State of South Carolina."[168] He observed that: "we can transact business here with a sense of dignity, as well as with comfort and convenience. It is elegant, appropriate and convenient. . . . This room I perceive is admirably adapted to the purpose of a court-room. As an auditorium I do not think I have ever been called on to speak in a hall more admirably arranged for the clear and easy use of the voice. The acoustic properties of the room are most excellent, and are as they

Joseph B. Kershaw. Courtesy, South
Carolina Historical Society,
Charleston.

should be to give ease to the speaker as well as ease and comfort to those whose duty
it is to hear what is said."[169]

Behind the courtroom the last two bays at the west end of the second floor were
divided into three offices for the judge, the circuit solicitor, and the stenographer of
the court. The floor of the judge's room was covered with a Brussels carpet while
those of the solicitor and stenographer were laid with a red and white cocoa matting. As with the office spaces below, these private chambers were equipped with
wash basins and running water.

As before, the jury rooms and the library of the Charleston Law Society were
located on the newly reconfigured third floor. This level was divided into five rooms
with a long corridor running longitudinally through the center of the building. Two
were used as jury rooms, two others served as storage for old records, and the fifth
provided a home for the Law Society. In a large apartment at the west end, the society had its library and meeting room.[170]

Throughout the building new woodwork was added and other improvements
made. Products of the sash-and-blind woodworking machinery of the Hall Manu-
facturing Company of Charleston, all the entrance doors, newel posts, handrails,
and balusters were made of walnut and must have looked much like those that still
survive in the City Hall, which had been remodeled in 1882. The earlier window
seats were removed, and the reworked openings received new two-light sash and

Staircase, Charleston City Hall. Photograph by Katherine Saunders, Historic Charleston Foundation, 1998.

surrounds painted a dark yellow with brown graining. To provide extra light for the third-floor rooms, the sills of the windows at this level were lowered to create large rectangular openings. At the same time, the niches that graced the second and eighth bays on the Broad Street facade were replaced by windows to light the office spaces on each of these floors, a change that lessened the architectural significance of this elevation. In the course of this work, many of the late-eighteenth-century floor-boards were removed and replaced by narrower ones of near uniform width. Rather than discard this material, a number of the old ones were reused as furring strips for new lathing and plaster. This reused flooring appeared in the southeast fireplace opening on the ground floor where the projecting chimney mass was cut back to the plane of the transverse wall. Here as in other rooms, the old open fireplace was closed off and replaced with a steam radiator heating system, which was vented by flues and supplied by a furnace in a newly excavated basement. Fragmentary evidence of this heating system has survived in the form of a chase cut into the rear wall of the northeast ground-floor room.

The job of creating a unified and logical courthouse, one that provided ample office space for the growing bureaucracy and a large courtroom and jury rooms to suit modern practices, had been accomplished. It was a logical plan whose antecedents dated back to the designs devised by Robert Mills in the 1820s. The extensive renovations were praised by one local chronicler who lauded the work as "very handsome . . . perfectly lighted and ventilated, and in every respect well

adapted to its uses."[171] It was adorned with costly new materials shaped in the lat- 75
est fashion, equipped with modern plumbing, heating, and lighting, and made efficient for the judicial needs of the 1880s, but at the cost of destroying the
architectural logic and grand spaces of the original building. From civic monument
to functional office, the symbolic significance of the building had been sacrificed on
the altar of bureaucratic efficiency.

A NEW FACADE

Transformation of the building in the pursuit of functional office space had a
detrimental effect on the outside of the building. The clarity of the late-eighteenth-
century Palladian design was severely compromised with the rotation of its orientation. Prominent elements that once expressed the civic importance of the building
and provided a sense of orientation were either obliterated or deliberately obscured.
The arcaded, three-bay pedimented projection on the Broad Street facade no longer
symbolized the formal entrance into a grand central stair hall but merely lit ground-
floor rooms. The Victorian renovations also dramatically altered the facade's proportions. The lowering of the third-story windows provided more light for offices

Charleston County Bench and Bar, 1899. Courtesy, Historic Charleston Foundation.

Granite frontispiece, east elevation, 1883, Edward Viett, sculptor. As part of the reorientation of the plan of the courthouse, the east doorway was made the primary entrance and a new frontispiece added to accentuate its importance. Ground-floor rustication was added at the same time. Photograph by Willie Graham, Colonial Williamsburg Foundation, 1993.

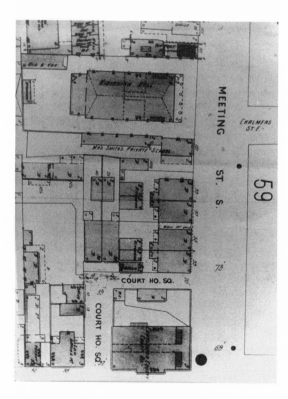

Sanborn Insurance Map, 1884. In this map the maker drew the new floor plan of the renovated courthouse with a stair hall adjacent to the main entrance on Meeting Street and a central corridor with small offices opening off of it. Courtesy, South Carolina Historical Society, Charleston.

A late-nineteenth-century view of the courthouse shows the extent of the 1883 renovations. The third-floor windows were lowered, new sashes were installed in all windows, and rustication was added to the ground floor. Courtesy, Historic Charleston Foundation.

but diminished the subtle visual hierarchy of floors. Before the 1883 renovations, the larger second floor windows signified the prominence of the courtroom floor. The smaller third-floor windows expressed the secondary importance of its offices and meeting rooms. This distinction now diminished.

The Victorian remodelers recognized that the removal of the primary entrance from Broad to Meeting Street required a bold new architectural solution to express this reorientation on the exterior. Edward T. Viett's granite frontispiece on the Meeting Street entrance provided a new focus of attention on the shorter side of the building. Removal of the south facade niches not only provided more light for the new offices but also lessened the impact of this elevation. Perhaps to downplay the importance of the central pavilion on the Broad Street facade, the entire ground-floor story was rusticated, repeating the pattern that previously had accentuated only the front arcade. To accomplish this, the remodelers cut into the original brickwork, creating splayed horizontal and vertical channels. The two string courses that had punctuated the upper levels were also removed, the uppermost one to allow for the enlargement of the third-floor window openings. Above the ground-floor rustication, the upper stories were painted and shaded in imitation of ashlar stonework. The most radical changes took place at the back of the building. The removal of the

78   central stair necessitated the reworking of the window openings in the north wall. The original Venetian window, along with the smaller compass-headed and lunette openings above it and the four flanking stair-landing windows, were all bricked up and covered with stucco. In their place three windows, matching their neighbors to the east and west, were inserted at the second- and third-floor levels. At least two ground-floor windows were inserted in the central section and matched the location of those above them. The old doors that once opened into the yard were blocked, and a new one was inserted in the center bay.

Finally, the courthouse yard also suffered at the hands of the Victorian remodeling. The ornamented brick wall that extended around the edge of the lot and linked the three outbuildings was partially torn down and rebuilt. The east and possibly west gate piers were also removed. In the northeast corner the old one-story brick privy was pulled down. Its twin in the northwest corner survived this assault, only to be removed with the construction of a rear courthouse wing in 1926. A high brick wall was built that extended uninterrupted around the east and north side of the lot until it reached the old two-story keeper's house.

ADDITIONS
AND RENOVATIONS,
1886–1989

The Earthquake Repairs, 1886

Two years after the radical alteration of the courthouse, a major earthquake struck Charleston, destroying many buildings and leaving others in a precarious condition. The courthouse survived this catastrophe but not without severe damage, especially to the west part of the building, which had been constructed over the fill of the colonial moat. An assessment of the damage for the Board of County Commissioners noted that the north wall was "slightly cracked," the south wall was "cracked at openings," the east wall was "badly cracked," and damage to the west wall was so thorough that it was recommended that "it should come down." The report suggested that the "east and west walls should come down, and [be] rebuilt with 1 ⅓ inch swivel anchor rods, 3 to each side."[172] Although the ensuing repairs did noth-

An 1886 view of the courthouse showing the cracks in the west wall caused by the recent earthquake. Courtesy, Historic Charleston Foundation.

80

View of the metal dentilated cornice and pediment constructed after the 1886 earthquake. Photograph by Jack Boucher, Historic American Buildings Survey, 1991.

ing to change the arrangement of the courthouse, the building underwent a number of alterations. Among the most significant was the rebuilding of the west wall at the second- and third-floor levels, as recommended by the damage assessors. At the third floor the removal of modern plaster revealed all new construction stretching from the outside jamb of the southernmost window to the opposite jamb of the northernmost one. At the second floor more of the original wall was retained. However, the central bay directly above the west door was entirely rebuilt, making it impossible to determine whether this opening had originally been a large window or door opening onto a balcony, as had its counterpart on the east wall. In contrast to the softer lime mortar used in the 1883 changes, workmen in 1886 laid the new work in a hard gray mortar consisting mainly of Portland cement with coarse black aggregate. Elsewhere in the building, cracks were patched, and the exterior received a new coat of stucco, lightly scored and tinted to resemble stone coursing.

The most notable permanent changes to the building appeared at the roof. The slate roof was removed after the earthquake and replaced with a standing seam metal covering. The old cornice, severely damaged during the earthquake, was replaced with a smaller metal cornice and a built-in gutter, proving detrimental to the proportions of the entablature. Instead of large modillion blocks, the new cornice had a small dentil course. The three pediments on the south, east, and west facades were slightly enlarged.

THE DEMAND FOR MORE SPACE

The 1926 Wing

The reconstitution of the courthouse in 1883 alleviated long-standing demands for a larger courtroom and more efficient offices. However, the radical restructuring of

the building served the court's requirements for only forty years. Voicing complaints   81
about the inadequacies of the old courthouse in a tone similar to that of grand juries
in the 1850s, a new generation of visiting judges and grand juries in the 1920s were
pressing for many needed repairs, modern conveniences, and additional space.
Finally, in the winter of 1926, the Charleston delegation to the General Assembly
prevailed upon the legislators to allocate $60,000 for the renovations.[173] With
money in hand, court and county officials moved quickly to develop plans and begin
construction. Under the direction of Judge Paul M. MacMillan, chairman of the
building commission, work began in May on the remodeling of the courthouse that
included the construction of a two-story wing adjoining the northwest corner of the
old building and extending the full depth of the courthouse yard. In order to make
room for the new wing, which would house a large courtroom on the second floor,
the surviving eighteenth-century privy in the northwest corner of the yard was
pulled down. However, the nearby keeper's house was retained.[174]

INTERIOR IMPROVEMENTS

The interior alterations of the courthouse were as sweeping as those of the 1880s.
Contractor M. L. Stephenson submitted the lowest bid for the general work and
began the process of gutting the old building in late spring. As a newspaper article
noted on 6 July: "The interior walls of the building have been torn away . . . the
work of replacing these petitions [sic] with new wooden supports has been com-
menced. All of the offices in the building will be installed with the latest conveniences when completed and will be a marked improvement over the old offices."[175]
Physical evidence suggests that the building was almost entirely stripped to the bare
walls, partitions removed and new ones inserted, creating smaller but more efficient
offices. In fact, so extensive was this remodeling that very little of the 1883 woodwork, or even that which may have remained from the 1790s, survived the construction. Many of the perimeter brick walls received a new hard coat of
cementitious plaster. On the internal corridor walls new plaster was laid over circu-
lar-sawn lath secured with wire nails to wooden furring strips. Much of this furring
was created from the late-eighteenth-century floorboards salvaged from other parts
of the building when the ground floor was completely laid with concrete. W. K.
Prause contracted to renew the plumbing, heating, and wiring.[176] Bathrooms were
added on the ground and second floors. In order to make the upper floors more
accessible, an elevator was inserted on the north wall near the center of the building. In addition a small staircase was erected in the central section of the building
where the grand staircase had once ascended, and a small window was inserted in
the north wall to light the landing.

Using modern materials, the new wing went up rapidly in the summer of 1926.
Although the walls were constructed of brick, massive steel I beams provided support for the large expanse of the second-floor courtroom, and the new openings cut
through the back wall of the original courthouse. To accommodate this wing, the
third-floor windows in the western third of the north wall were raised slightly above

A 1927 view of the courthouse. Note the colonial housekeeper's, or jailer's, house at the rear. Courtesy, Historic Charleston Foundation.

View across Washington Park looking west. This photograph was taken after the tornado of 1938. The two-story wing added in 1926 is visible just behind the housekeeper's, or jailer's, house. At the right is the Timrod Hotel, demolished in the 1960s to make room for a county office building. Courtesy, Charleston Library Society.

the new roof line. By constructing a large courtroom in the wing, the building commissioners intended the old section to be used mainly as office space. The only major external change to the appearance of the old building was the principal entry's return to Broad Street "as it was originally intended when the court house was first built and as it was until many years afterwards."[177] The "much improved and enlarged building" was reoccupied by court and county offices in late January 1927. The ground floor housed the clerk's office, the sheriff's office, and the offices of the two masters in equity. The second floor contained the main courtroom in the new wing as well as a judge's chamber, attorney's room, and probate court. A grand jury room, two petit jury rooms, a witness room, and several offices for court and county officials occupied the third floor of the old section.[178] With the thorough gutting of the original building and the addition of the two-story courtroom wing, Charleston officials took great satisfaction in bringing the courthouse into the twentieth century as they followed the general outline of a plan advanced in the middle of the previous century.

HOMAGE TO A CONFUSING PAST

The 1941 Expansion

The 1926 improvements, which were intended to meet long-term spatial requirements of the courts, lasted less than two decades. No sooner had officials learned to navigate their way through the maze of corridors than the familiar complaints of overcrowding were voiced once again. By the eve of World War II, many of the offices that had moved into the Fireproof Building in the 1820s had outgrown that venerable structure and were "hopelessly inadequate." In 1938 a committee made up of members of the local bar association recommended that, for the convenient functioning of the growing county government, all offices should be consolidated within an enlarged courthouse that would have fireproof offices to contain the expanding collection of records. The committee believed that this solution would "take care of the needs" of the county "for the next twenty years."

When plans were debated in late 1940 for expanding the courthouse, the logical solution to the courts' problems seemed to be in continuing the pattern established by the 1926 addition to the north. Charleston architect David B. Hyer devised a scheme to build a three-story wing across the remaining portion of the courthouse yard, raising the 1926 annex an extra story to match this new addition.[179] Recognizing the historical significance of the courthouse, Hyer carefully designed the Meeting Street facade of the new section to match the exterior appearance of the original building, thus preserving "the architectural lines of the old structure."[180] Whether or not he knew it, this approach followed the precedent prescribed in the ill-fated 1860 plan. However, the architect chose to copy the changes that had been made to the building during the 1883 renovations. Thus the new addition had elongated third-floor windows, rustication around the ground story, and a replica of the frontispiece erected on the Meeting Street entrance. Unfortunately this imitation of the Victorian changes only served to further obscure the logic of the original late-eighteenth-century design.

84

View of the back of the courthouse before the removal of the 1926 and 1941 additions in 1993. Photograph by Willie Graham, Colonial Williamsburg Foundation, 1991.

Nearly $80,000 was appropriated to complete this work as well as refurbish the older sections of the courthouse. Among the first steps was the demolition of the 1883 wall and the keeper's house, the last of the pre-Revolutionary period out-buildings that lined the back of the courthouse yard. A newspaper article observed that "its heavily quoined corners give it a quaint look, but its room is needed more than its company"—remarks that were to be repeated many times in coming decades when arguments were made for demolishing many of the city's historic structures.[181] In doubling the size of the Meeting Street facade, officials decided once again to de-emphasize the Broad Street elevation. A new granite doorway, matching the 1883 one carved by Edward Viett for the old building, was designed for the sec-ond major entrance on Meeting Street. This entrance led directly into a much-enlarged, fireproof clerk's office. The architect underscored this new approach by converting the Broad Street entrance into a window.

The 1941 design placed a large and well-lit courtroom on the third floor of the north wing. Hyer had to work within the limitation imposed by the twelve-foot height of the third floor in the old section when designing the new courtroom. To mitigate the claustrophobic effect of a flat, low ceiling in a large room, the architect devised a vaulted ceiling that stood seventeen feet in height in the center and pro-jected into the space of the roof. Four skylights provided additional light. In addi-tion to acoustical tiles made of Blendex, which improved the hearing in the courtroom, the greatest achievement was improved circulation routes within the building. Hyer's plan made it possible for the jury and prisoners to enter and leave

the courtroom "by a rear corridor, closed to the public, instead of having to walk   85
through the audience as they do now. This change will make it more difficult to
tamper with juries."[182]

In order to reach this new courtroom, a new but smaller staircase replaced the
1883 staircase in the east section of the old building. Two elevators were installed
on the south side of the longitudinal corridor in the old section of the building—one
near the Meeting Street door and the other next to the west entrance off Courthouse
Alley. These major changes and many minor ones, such as the installation of new
heating, plumbing, and electrical systems and the repartitioning of the old section,
destroyed more of the building's eighteenth-century fabric.

NEW PARTITIONS AND A NOD TO THE PAST

The 1968–69 Renovations
The renovations of 1941 served the county and courts for only a short period before
arguments arose once again for more space and better offices. After falling plaster
caused a "rain" of terror in the courthouse in late 1949, officials installed acoustical tile and brightened the appearance of most offices by covering many cracks with
a fresh coat of "spring green" paint.[183] Despite cosmetic changes and redecorating,
county and court officials finally came to the conclusion in the late 1950s that the
courthouse could not contain all their offices. A new building was needed, and the
courthouse itself required yet another reworking of its labyrinthian maze of offices
and corridors. By the mid-1960s, talk of abandoning the old building altogether
caused a stir among Charlestonians who had become increasingly aware of the cultural value of the city's historic buildings. In 1966 five hundred "lovers of
Charleston" sent a petition to the county council urging the enlargement of the

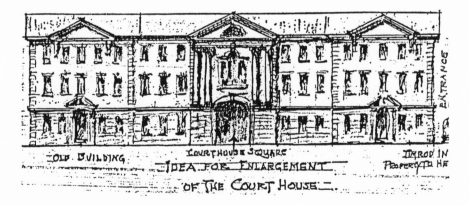

In the 1960s cramped conditions in the courthouse led to renewed calls for a new addition
to the courthouse. Charleston historian and architect Samuel G. Stoney proposed an addition
to the north that would have more than doubled the size of the building. Stoney's design
was rejected, but the crowding led to the construction of an office building north of Courthouse Alley on the site of the Timrod Hotel. *Charleston News and Courier,* 4 April 1966.

86   courthouse in a manner that would be "in keeping with its eighteenth-century architecture." Samuel G. Stoney, architect and historian of Charleston's early architecture, submitted a proposal on behalf of the group that more than doubled the size of the building. Stoney's design called for the construction of a new building where the Timrod Hotel stood on the north side of Courthouse Square. The office would replicate the features of the 1883 facade. He proposed to link the new building to the old by means of a pedimented projection supported by paired columns above the street entrance.[184]

Stoney's ambitious design was not followed, but the petitioners' plea to retain the old courthouse and to make new construction conform to the architectural character of the old building was well received. More than one-half million dollars was appropriated for renovations to the courthouse in 1968 in conjunction with the construction of a county office building on the lot to the north of Courthouse Square. The architectural firm of Archie Myers and David Parrott submitted designs for the new work, which included a courtroom in the southern end of the original building's central section. Directly above, a larger courtroom occupied the entire central section of the original second floor. Reopening this area raised the old problem of supporting the upper floor over a large second-floor space.[185] In this case two pairs of steel girders were inserted in the locations of earlier wood members, borne on columns that ran to new footings in the basement.

The work also renewed plumbing, mechanical, electrical, and communications systems for which portions of the crawl space were excavated to create new mechanical rooms. At the same time, the 1941 stair was superseded by new concrete staircases in fire-rated enclosures at both ends of the old structure. Opposite each of these enclosures, a new elevator provided access to the upper floors. The solution to overcrowding appeared to be yet another subdivision, as the old section and the twentieth-century additions were shuffled into new arrangements. A report on the renovations noted that "the old building is virtually gutted and a new building constructed inside the walls," which meant that old fabric was once again destroyed.[186] Many offices and the principal courtrooms received yet another cosmetic makeover, this time with vinyl wall covering grained in imitation of walnut and applied over earlier layers of plaster, Blendex, and Sheetrock. Whether courtroom or cloakroom, no distinction was made in the finish treatment of various rooms, thus obliterating any symbolic significance architectural finishes might have played in distinguishing a hierarchy of court spaces.

Recognizing that the previous renovations had obscured many of the most interesting features of the 1790s exterior, this generation of building commissioners made a partial effort to restore some of the earlier elements. For example, the location of the old Broad Street entry was indicated by replacing the 1941 window with a pair of false doors in the Eastlake style of the 1880s—this to match the existing doors of the east and west entries. In addition to noting the location of the original Broad Street entrance, the architects sought to recreate the 1790s niches on the building's Broad Street front even though the 1880s ground-floor rustication was

Courthouse showing the south and east facades, 1991. The addition on the rear on the Meeting Street facade was added in 1941 following the design of architect David Hyer. The niches on the Broad Street facade were rebuilt during the 1969 renovations. Photograph by Willie Graham, Colonial Williamsburg Foundation.

still in place. Since the third-floor window openings remained taller than they were originally, it was necessary to elongate the new recesses on this level. On the north side of the 1941 wing, an entry was created to handle traffic between the courthouse and the new county office building. However, the north wall was not revamped in any other manner to reflect the increased importance of this facade with the construction of the county office and landscaped courtyard just across the alley. The partial renovations of 1968–69 provided a glimpse of what had been destroyed by later alterations, but it was a muddled effort that neither restored the intentions of the 1790s design nor completely effaced the effects of the 1880s reorientation of the building.

CONCLUSION

Making Sense of the Past

In September 1989 Hurricane Hugo devastated Charleston and the surrounding lowcountry. High winds ripped through the city, tearing off roofs, blowing down chimneys, and demolishing many less substantial structures. The accompanying rainstorm inundated hundreds of dwellings, stores, and public buildings. The storm left its mark on the courthouse as it rent the roof covering and emptied thousands of gallons of water into the offices and courtrooms below. As court and county offices moved to drier venues, the county debated what to do with the wrecked building. Even before the storm forced the issue, officials realized that the courthouse was beginning to show signs of serious deterioration. Flaking stucco on the outside and antiquated electrical and mechanical systems indicated that the renovations of the late 1960s were beginning to wear out.

The disaster wrought by Hugo provided an opportunity for the county to consider the future of the court system in Charleston. It clearly recognized that the courthouse would require yet another thorough renovation if it were to meet the needs of a new century. Yet the demand for more offices for various members of the court, the desire to provide courtroom access for the disabled, and the installation of improved security systems for those awaiting trial and attending court sessions meant that substantial alterations would have to be made to the building. Once again it seemed unlikely that the courthouse could contain all that was asked of it. Even so, an initial set of recommendations made to the county by an architectural conservation firm called for simply tidying up the facade to the period 1886–1941 and reshuffling the interior once again. However, at the urging of Historic Charleston Foundation, another study of the building by architectural historians in 1991 showed that significant parts of the original fabric still survived beneath layers of alterations, but with each new renovation, more and more of that past was being destroyed. The recommendations made to the county council suggested a new tack.[187]

Rather than subject the building to another remodeling that would only rearrange the same amount of space and add to the confusion about the historical importance and architectural significance of the courthouse, the Charleston County Council agreed to proceed in an entirely different fashion for two reasons. First, the availability of a new building site near the courthouse alleviated one of the most pressing problems—that of space. The prospect of a second court building made it unnecessary to fit all the offices and courtrooms back into the historic structure. Second, the old courthouse could be restored to its late-eighteenth-century appearance with reasonable assurance of accuracy. Evidence for many of the missing elements of the early facade and plan were found after careful scrutiny of the historic fabric and documents.

As a result, and with the urging of the Friends of the Charleston County Courthouse—a broad-based organization of preservationists, attorneys, and government officials concerned with the fate and appearance of the building—the council voted in September 1991 to remove the twentieth-century additions and restore the external appearance of the courthouse to the period when it was first used as the county courthouse in the late eighteenth century. It also approved the reconfiguration of the original circulation pattern with the reconstruction of the central staircase and lobby and the reopening of the principal Broad Street entrance.[188] This bold step was taken in order to arrest the continued abuse of one of the most historic buildings in the state. By calling attention to the significance of the courthouse through its restoration to its early appearance, the council hoped Charlestonians would once again appreciate the value of public architecture in defining the civic aspirations of the community. The decision to restore the courthouse and erect a new judicial center nearby not only was an important victory for the preservation of this historic building but also confirmed the county's commitment to retain a vital institution downtown. Rather than moving the courts out of downtown to a more centralized location further up the peninsula, as some had urged, the council's action also ensured the continued economic viability of many commercial establishments dependent upon the business generated by the courts and the legal profession along Broad Street and other parts of the Civic Square neighborhood.

In the summer of 1993 the first steps in this undertaking began with the demolition of the twentieth-century additions and an archaeological survey of the rear courtyard. However, after this initial step the courthouse restoration encountered a number of delays, not the least of which was a debate over the mounting costs of the project, including a quixotic attempt to reinforce the fabric of the building to make it earthquake proof. Questions arose about the necessity of completely restoring the late-eighteenth-century facade. Some members of the community and council favored a piecemeal effort that reconstructed some features but eliminated others deemed too costly, a solution that had been tried with unfortunate results in 1969. Eventually these differences were worked out among the various political factions, and the members of county council—many of them newly elected to office—voted once again in 1997 to proceed with the restoration, which moved forward slowly over the next four years. By the beginning of the twenty-first century, for the first time in more than one hundred years, those who lived in Charleston, as well as the thousands of visitors who flocked to this historic city, could appreciate the architectural qualities that had made the courthouse one of the most important buildings of the new republic.

The 1926 and 1941 wings were demolished in the summer of 1993, leading to the restoration of the courthouse to its late-eighteenth-century appearance. Photograph by Jim Wigley, 1993.

View of the back of the courthouse showing the proposed renovation of the north wall. Photograph by Willie Graham, Colonial Williamsburg Foundation, 1993.

THE FUTURE OF THE PAST   91

Despite the many vicissitudes that the building has suffered in its nearly two and one-half centuries of existence, the county courthouse still plays an important part in the cultural life of Charleston. A tangible reminder of the state's colonial heritage, the building is one of only a handful of surviving colonial statehouses. For this reason alone, the structure is of national importance. Many of the dramatic events that precipitated South Carolina's dramatic struggle for independence from Great Britain occurred within the walls of this building. After the removal of state government from Charleston and the fire of 1788, the building emerged in a new and prominent role as the county and federal district courthouse. For a number of years in the early nineteenth century, members of the U.S. Supreme Court sat in circuit sessions in the northeast room where colonial governors once proclaimed the authority of the British Crown. In the same courtroom in the early 1830s, South Carolinians challenged the authority of the federal government over tariffs, setting the stage for a more bitter and tragic struggle over the meaning of national sovereignty thirty years later. Serving for more than two hundred years as the focus of the legal community of the city and surrounding countryside, the courthouse has witnessed many important events in Charlestonians' quest for justice and interpretation of the rule of law. Few other courthouses in the country can claim such a venerable and illustrious lineage.

A fragment of the late-eighteenth-century exterior modillion cornice. Several pieces of the Aquia sandstone cornice erected in the early 1790s by Robert Given were reused as fill in the upper portions of the west wall following the earthquake of 1886. A new metal cornice replaced the sandstone one during the repairs. This fragment still retains several layers of paint and was in remarkably good condition with few signs of wear. The cornice work is visible in the 1883 photograph on page 1. Photograph by Carl Lounsbury, 2000.

NOTES

1. In *This Is Charleston,* a survey of the architecturally significant structures in the city published in 1944, the courthouse received a Nationally Important designation, the highest category awarded. Samuel Stoney, ed., *This is Charleston* (Charleston: Carolina Art Association, 1944).

2. William Gilmore Simms, "Charleston," *Harper's New Monthly Magazine,* June 1857, quoted in Beatrice St. Julien Ravenel, *Architects of Charleston* (1945; reprint, Columbia: University of South Carolina Press, 1992), 75.

3. Robert Rosen, conversation with author, 31 July 1996.

4. The local newspaper noted that "the CORNER STONE of our STATE HOUSE, was laid, by his Excellency the Governor, and a Sum of Money thereon: After him, the several Members of His Majesty's Council and the Assembly, the Commissioners, and other Gentlemen who attended the Governor, laid each a Brick in the proper manner." *South Carolina Gazette*, 2 July 1753, p. 1, col. 1–2. For an earlier version of this introductory section, see Carl Lounsbury, "The Dynamics of Architectural Design in Eighteenth-Century Charleston and the Lowcountry," *Exploring Everyday Landscapes: Perspectives in Vernacular Architecture,* VII, ed. Annmarie Adams and Sally McMurray (Knoxville: University of Tennessee Press, 1997), 58–72.

5. George Williams, *St. Michael's, Charleston, 1751–1951* (Columbia: University of South Carolina Press, 1951), 14, 151.

6. W. Stitt Robinson, *James Glen: From Scottish Provost to Royal Governor of South Carolina* (Westport, Conn.: Greenwood Press, 1996), 69.

7. For a study of cultural and political life of Charleston during this period, see George C. Rogers, Jr., *Charleston in the Age of the Pinckneys* (Columbia: University of South Carolina Press, 1980), and Walter J. Fraser, Jr., *Charleston! Charleston!: The History of a Southern City* (Columbia: University of South Carolina Press), 1989.

8. John J. McCusker and Russell R. Menard, *The Economy of British America, 1607–1789* (Chapel Hill: University of North Carolina Press, 1985), 179.

9. *South Carolina Gazette,* 9 August 1735, p. 4, col. 1.

10. See Richard Waterhouse, "The Responsible Gentry of Colonial South Carolina: A Study in Local Government, 1670–1770," *Town and Country: Essays on the Structure of Local Government in the American Colonies,* ed. Bruce C. Daniels (Middletown, Conn.: Wesleyan University Press, 1978), 160–85.

11. The Commons House of Assembly appointed a number of parish and other special commissioners to perform a variety of functions, such as maintaining the roads, building fortifications, and overseeing the market in Charleston. Some commissions became self-sustaining oligarchies after initial appointments were made by the assembly. On the importance of commissions, see Walter Edgar, *South Carolina: A History* (Columbia: University of South Carolina Press, 1998), 127–29.

94   12. Mark A. DeWolfe Howe, ed., "Journal of Josiah Quincy, Junior, 1773," *Proceedings of the Massachusetts Historical Society* 49 (1915–1916): 441–51, 455.

13. Johann David Schoepf, *Travels in the Confederation (1783–1784),* ed. and trans. Alfred J. Morrison (New York: Burt Franklin, 1968), 2:167–68.

14. Daniel Defoe, *A Tour through the Whole Island of Great Britain* (1724; reprint, New York: Penguin Books, 1978), 261, 368.

15. Letter from Mrs. Margaret Kennett to Mrs. Thomas Brett, 20 January 1725, *South Carolina Historical Magazine* 61 (1960): 15.

16. One such immigrant from the British Isles was Samuel Cardy, a builder from Dublin who came to Charleston in the early 1750s. Shortly after his arrival he was entrusted with the construction of St. Michael's Church. See Kenneth Severens, "Emigration and Provincialism: Samuel Cardy's Architectural Career in the Atlantic World," *Eighteenth Century Ireland* 5 (1990): 21–36.

17. *South Carolina Gazette and Country Journal,* 22 August 1769.

18. Howe, "Journal of Josiah Quincy, Junior, 1773," 444–45.

19. In 1789 a contract specified the construction of a "well-finished dwelling house commonly called a single house, three stories high . . . twenty-two feet wide or thereabouts and forty-six feet long or thereabouts, with two rooms on a floor and an entry leading to a stair case in or near the centre of the said house nine foot wide in the clear . . . with two stacks of chimneys so as to allow one fire Place in each room." Charleston County Land Records Book R. For a discussion of the single house, see Bernard Herman, "The Charleston Single House," in Jonathan Poston, *The Buildings of Charleston: A Guide to the City's Architecture* (Columbia: University of South Carolina Press, 1997), 37–41.

20. William Waller Hening, *The Statutes at Large, Being a Collection of All the Laws of Virginia* (New York: R. & W. & G. Bartow, 1823), 2:204.

21. Quoted in Maurice Howard, "Classicism and Civic Architecture in Renaissance England," *Albion's Classicism: The Visual Arts in Britain, 1550–1660,* ed. Lucy Gent (New Haven: Yale University Press, 1995), 40. See also Mark Girourard, *The English Town: A History of Urban Life* (New Haven: Yale University Press, 1990).

22. Charles Fraser, *Reminiscences of Charleston* (1854; reprint, Charleston: Garnier & Company, 1969), 101.

23. *South Carolina Gazette,* 7 February 1761, p. 2, col. 2.

24. *South Carolina Gazette and Country Journal,* 13 August 1771, p. 2, col. 3.

25. Peter Borsay, *The English Urban Renaissance: Culture and Society in the Provincial Town, 1660–1770* (Oxford: Oxford University Press, 1989).

26. Quoted in "Remarks by George C. Rogers," in "Saving a Landmark," a symposium sponsored by Friends of the Charleston County Courthouse, 24 May 1990, 16.

27. "Acts of the Council in Assembly, 1749–1756, Act: 13," CO5/420, Great Britain Public Record Office, London.

28. Walter Edgar and Louise Bailey, *Biographical Directory of the South Carolina House of Representatives,* vol. 2, *The Commons House of Assembly, 1692–1775* (Columbia: University of South Carolina Press, passim, 1984); Edward McCrady, *The History of South Carolina under the Royal Government, 1719–1776* (1899; republished, New York: Russell & Russell, 1969), 799–803.

29. In designing his dwelling, Pinckney specified that the second-floor rooms be wainscoted in the same manner as in fellow commissioner and justice James Graeme's house. Rogers, *Charleston in the Age of the Pinckneys,* 59, 68.

30. Williams, *St. Michael's, Charleston, 1751–1951*, 12–13.

31. Samuel Prioleau, Jr., was appointed clerk of the statehouse building commission. In that capacity, he probably scheduled meetings, posted public notices for hiring workmen and purchasing materials, and received proposals. He served in a similar capacity for the commissioners of St. Michael's church. See, for example, *South Carolina Gazette*, 24 June 1751, p. 3, col. 2; 15 July 1751, Postscript, p. 1, col. 1.

32. In 1768 Peter and John Horlbeck received £1,250 for "Rough Casting the State House." *Journal of the Commons House of Assembly*, no. 37, pt. 2, 23 February 1768, 526–27, South Carolina Department of Archives and History.

33. New South Associates, "Restoration Archaeology at the Charleston County Courthouse Site (38CH 1498) Charleston, South Carolina" (report submitted to Liollio Associates, Inc., September 1993), 61–63.

34. George Milligen Johnston, *A Short Description of the Province of South-Carolina* (1770; reprinted in Robert L. Meriwether, ed., *South Caroliniana* [Columbia: University of South Carolina Press, 1951]).

35. Close inspection of the original relieving arches in the center section of the ground floor reveals that the front wall was initially two feet, ten inches thick, matching the present thickness of neighboring walls. This suggests that if there was originally an arcade, the brickwork for it was not tied into the main walls but constructed separately, or that it was integrally connected but hacked away after the fire when the present arcade was constructed. Both possibilities seem highly improbable. Investigations in 2000 proved the present arcade was added in the rebuilding that followed the fire of 1788.

36. "Charleston, S.C., in 1774 as Described by an English Traveller," reprinted in *The Colonial South Carolina Scene: Contemporary View, 1697–1774*, ed. H. Roy Merrens (Columbia: University of South Carolina Press, 1977), 282.

37. All door and window heads were the same height. The Meeting Street doorway, opening into a transverse corridor, and the west doorway, opening into the large courtroom, were originally wider and were flat headed.

38. The responsibility of furnishing the new statehouse was in the hands of another committee composed of William Bull, Jr., William Wragg, George Saxby, James Michie, and Othniel Beale from the council and Henry Middleton, John Rattray, Thomas Middleton, Luke Stoutenburgh, Peter Manigault, Charles Pinckney, and John Graeme from the Commons House. Terry Lipscomb, ed., *The Journal of the Commons House of Assembly, 1755–1757* (Columbia: University of South Carolina Press, 1989), 198, 201.

39. Ibid., 155.

40. Terry Lipscomb and R. Nicholas Olsberg, eds., *The Journal of the Commons House of Assembly, 1751–1752* (Columbia: University of South Carolina Press, 1977), 151; Lipscomb, *The Journal of the Commons House of Assembly, 1755–1757*, 154–55.

41. Evidence for this assumption is inconclusive. In the summer of 1993, test excavations by New South Associates beneath the modern concrete floor of the lobby area exposed a disturbed layer of soil nearly four feet deep that contained artifacts dating from the first half of the eighteenth century. The soil probably was used as fill during the construction of the building. The discovery of a builder's trench for a brick foundation wall running from north to south through this lobby could argue for the presence of a wooden floor. Intermediate walls could have been used to support girders for framing a wooden floor. Yet, by the middle of the nineteenth century, the lobby of the courthouse was paved with stone. At some time in the 1850s, a grand jury observed that "noise in the lobby" disrupted court business and that "this evil

96   might be remedied to a considerable extent by laying down cocoa matting upon the flag pavement of the lobby and upon the staircase leading to the second story." New South Associates, "Restoration Archaeology at the Charleston County Courthouse Site," 50–51; General Assembly Papers ND 00008 01, Columbia, South Carolina Department of Archives and History.

42. This conclusion is similar to that of John Milner Associates in "Charleston County Courthouse: A Historic Structure Report on the Architectural Development and Historical Alterations to the Building" (report prepared for Liollio Associates, Inc., January 1991), 42, fig. 20.

43. T. P. Harrison, ed., "Journal of a Voyage to Charlestown in So. Carolina by Pelatiah Webster in 1756," *Publications of the South Carolina Historical Society* (Charleston: The Society, 1898), 5.

44. Two of these doors are located under the corner stair landings. The door directly below the east landing may date from the initial period of construction whereas the one beneath the west landing clearly dates to the rebuilding that followed the disastrous fire in 1788. The sole surviving window, like the other two doors, was blocked during renovations in 1883, when the stair location was moved and the fenestration was regularized on the back wall.

45. Archaeological testing of the courtyard did not discover any fencing or other indication of a subdivision of this space. New South Associates, "Restoration Archaeology at the Charleston County Courthouse Site," 84–85.

46. In January 1994 further archaeological investigation of this area revealed an earlier circular cistern, about fifteen feet in diameter, just north of this larger cistern. Charleston County Auditor's Records, Box 6, 1877–1888, Vouchers of County Funds, 1877–1878, Office of the County Commissioners, South Carolina Department of Archives and History.

47. The vaulting is likely to have carried stone paving. Fragments of Aquia sandstone pavers were recovered in the rubble after the destruction of the twentieth-century additions in the summer of 1993 and in January 1994. It is unlikely that this vaulted platform had a superstructure supporting a piazza or portico, as no visual or documentary evidence of its presence has come to light. Another problem with the possibility of a one- or two-story piazza is the relationship between the window openings and any upper floor and roof framing of this feature, which would cut across some or all of the apertures. In addition there would have been no access from the upper floors of the building onto the upper story of a piazza.

48. *Journal of the Commons House of Assembly,* no. 37, pt. 2, 23 February 1768, 526–27.

49. All three buildings and the enclosing wall are clearly delineated on a deed map drawn up in 1788 and on a map of the town made the same year but published in 1790. See Charleston County Deed Book, vol. 6G, 32–33, July 1788; Edmund Petrie, *Ichnography of Charleston, South Carolina, at the Request of Adam Tunno, Esq. for the use of the Phoenix Fire-Company of London,* January 1790.

50. In 1768 Peter and John Horlbeck were paid £321.15.6 for "paving the West, North and East sides" of the statehouse. Additional payments totaling £160.4.3 were made to an unspecified workman, perhaps one of the Horlbecks, for "a Well in the Yard, Carting earth to and leveling the Yard, sinking a Drain there from to the Common Sewer, laying a kerb, Grate, etc." In the same year Bernard Beekman was paid £61.4.0 for "pumps at the State House." *Journal of the Commons House of Assembly,* no. 37, pt. 2, 23 February 1768, 526–27; South Carolina General Tax Receipts and Payments, 1761–1769, Columbia, South Carolina Department of Archives and History, 140.

51. This cistern, which had neither a lining nor a masonry floor, may have functioned as a fire well in the late eighteenth and early nineteenth centuries. Its main purpose would have

been to collect and store rainwater that was channeled from a gutter on the roof of the keeper's house. New South Associates, "Restoration Archaeology at the Charleston County Courthouse Site," 52–56.

52. Unfortunately the transverse wall has been demolished at this location, leaving no evidence to verify this assumption.

53. There is strong circumstantial evidence for a chimney in the courtroom in this position following the fire of 1788 and the subsequent transformation of the building into the Charleston County Courthouse. To support the courtroom ceiling, a large summer beam was inserted spanning from the west wall of the building to the west partition separating the courtroom from the stair passage. This beam, which has survived but was moved from its original location during the renovations of 1883, probably spanned the courtroom at the midpoint between the back north wall and the southern partition wall separating the jury room from the courtroom. The underside of the beam has plaster lath marks along its entire length except the last two and one-half feet of the east end, where they abruptly stop. These ghost marks reveal the extension of the ceiling to a point where it terminated against the now-destroyed chimney stack.

54. *Journal of the Commons House of Assembly*, January 1765–August 1765, 16 July 1765, 87.

55. South Carolina General Tax Receipts and Payments, 1761–1769, 140.

56. On 27 June 1758 the building commissioners reported that there was a quantity of material left over from the construction of the statehouse, including "a parcel of paving stones." Although archaeological evidence suggests that the lobby entrance was floored with plank rather than stone, it is not clear whether stone was used elsewhere, such as the courtroom. *Journal of the Commons House of Assembly of South Carolina from the 4th day of February to the 20th day of August 1760*, CO5/473, Public Records Office, London, 58. For a study of Virginia courthouses, see Carl Lounsbury, "The Structure of Justice: The Courthouses of Colonial Virginia," *Perspectives in Vernacular Architecture*, III, ed. Thomas Carter and Bernard Herman (Columbia: University of Missouri Press, 1989), 214–26.

57. *South Carolina Gazette and Country Journal*, 7 November 1771, p. 3, col. 1.

58. For a study of the rise of the legal profession in South Carolina, see Hoyt Paul Canady, Jr., "Gentlemen of the Bar: Lawyers in Colonial South Carolina" (Ph.D. dissertation, University of Tennessee, 1979).

59. Canady, Jr., "Gentlemen of the Bar," 259–61, 290.

60. Johnston, *A Short Description of the Province of South-Carolina*, 35.

61. *Journal of the Commons House of Assembly*, no. 32, 10 February 1758, 104–5, Columbia, South Carolina Department of Archives and History.

62. *Journal of the Commons House of Assembly*, no. 32, 19 January 1759, 48.

63. Lipscomb, *The Journal of the Commons House of Assembly, 1755–1757*, 12 March 1756, 138.

64. Johnston, *A Short Description of the Province of South-Carolina*, 35.

65. Harrison, "Journal of a Voyage to Charlestown in So. Carolina by Pelatiah Webster in 1765," 5.

66. The firm of Weyman and Carne was paid £23 in 1764 for "A Glass for the Speakers Chamber." South Carolina General Tax Receipts and Payments, 1761–1769, 87.

67. For a discussion of the struggle over legislative power between the two bodies, see M. Eugene Sirmans, *Colonial South Carolina: A Political History, 1663–1763* (Chapel Hill: University of North Carolina Press, 1966), 279–81, 295–314.

98   68. *South Carolina Gazette,* 24 June 1756, p. 3, col. 1.

69. *South Carolina Gazette,* 7 February 1761, p. 2, col. 1.

70. *The South Carolina and American General Gazette,* 10 July 1777, p. 3, col. 1.

71. Robert M. Weir, *Colonial South Carolina: A History* (Millwood, N.Y.: KTO Press, 1983), 246. For a view of the old council chamber on Bay Street, see *Prospect of Charles Town,* from a watercolor by Bishop Roberts 1735–1739, engraved by W. H. Toms, 9 June 1749.

72. Theodora J. Thompson, ed., *Journals of the House of Representatives, 1783–1784* (Columbia: University of South Carolina Press, 1977), 100.

73. Christopher Lee, "The Transformation of the Executive in Post-Revolutionary South Carolina," *South Carolina Historical Magazine* 93 (April 1992): 85.

74. *Journal of the Proceedings of the Honourable the Upper House of Assembly, 1755–1756,* 4 April 1756, 50, Columbia, South Carolina Department of Archives and History.

75. A. S. Salley, *The State Houses of South Carolina, 1751–1936* (Columbia: Historical Commission of South Carolina, n.d.), 5–6. Among the craftsmen who had worked on the statehouse, bricklayer Anthony Toomer, blockmaker Bernard Beekman, painters George Flagg and Benjamin Hawes, and upholsterer Edward Weyman actively promoted the radical cause during the 1760s and 1770s. See Richard Walsh, *Charleston's Sons of Liberty: A Study of the Artisans, 1763–1789* (Columbia: University of South Carolina Press, 1959).

76. David Stoddard was paid £55.17.19 for the New England pine. *Journal of the Commons House of Assembly,* no. 37, pt. 2, 23 February 1768, 526–27. For a synopsis of Woodin's career, see Geoffrey Beard and Christopher Gilbert, eds., *Dictionary of English Furniture Makers, 1660–1840* (Leeds: W. S. Maney & Sons, Ltd., 1986), 999.

77. *South Carolina Gazette,* 12 October 1765, p. 1, col. 2.

78. *Journal of the Commons House of Assembly,* no. 37, pt. 2, 23 February 1768, 526–27.

79. In 1767 Thomas and Roger Smith were paid £40.10 for "sundries" for "curtain to King's Picture in the Council Chamber." Edward Weyman was paid £28.10 for "making a Curtain to the King's Picture." South Carolina General Tax Receipts and Payments, 1760–1769, Columbia, South Carolina Department of Archives and History, 123. This may have been the portrait of King George I that Charles Fraser saw around 1800 gathering dust in the former magazine near St. Philip's Church. Along with this royal portrait, Fraser noticed another depicting Queen Anne. Now hanging in City Hall is a fragment of an eighteenth-century painting of a woman's hand clasping an orb, said to be part of that portrait of Anne that also may have hung in the statehouse. Fraser, *Reminiscences of Charleston,* 29–30.

80. In 1768 the public treasury paid Laurens, Motte, & Co. £865.19.0 for a "pair of stove grates" and "sundries for the courtroom." This suggests that perhaps the other grate may have been installed in the lobby fireplace. South Carolina General Tax Receipts and Payments, 1761–1769, 140.

81. *Journal of the Commons House of Assembly,* no. 32, 21 April 1758, 162; Thomas Cooper, ed. *The Statutes at Large of South Carolina,* 4 (Columbia: A. S. Johnson, 1838), 72.

82. Bradford L. Rauschenberg, "The Royal Governor's Chair: Evidence of the Furnishing of South Carolina's First State House," *Journal of the Early Southern Decorative Arts* 6 (November 1980): 17–27.

83. *Journal of the Commons House of Assembly,* no. 34, 21 May 1761, 82–83.

84. Johnston, *A Short Description of the Province of South-Carolina,* 35.

85. Harrison, "Journal of a Voyage to Charlestown in So. Carolina by Pelatiah Webster in 1765," 5.

86. Once the Commons House moved into its new quarters, it ordered that "a mace, robes for the speakers, and a gown for the clerk" be purchased or procured in England. *Journal of the Commons House of Assembly, 1755–1756*, 3 April 1756, 95.

87. Howe, "Journal of Josiah Quincy, Junior, 1773," 451–52. The mace still survives. It was made in London in 1756 by Magdalen Feline. It was described in a newspaper account from the late nineteenth century as being made of silver, gilded, and measuring four feet in length. A sliding cylinder at the staff allowed the mace to extend to six or seven feet when it was carried before the speaker. It had four devices on the main part of it, including the royal coat of arms. The article also mentions the sword of state, which was a "blade of fine steel some five feet in length, with a hilt of silver." *Charleston News and Courier*, 20 October 1882, p. 1, col. 7. The sword of state was carried by the provost marshal during the ceremony at the statehouse proclaiming King George III in 1761. *South Carolina Gazette*, 7 February 1761, p. 2, col. 2. See also A. S. Salley, *The Mace of the House of Representatives of the State of South Carolina* (Columbia: The State Company, 1917); and *Seals and Symbols of South Carolina Government Through Three Centuries* (Columbia: Columbia Museums of Art and Science, 1982).

88. On the history of the Pitt statue, see Jonathan Poston, "Statue of William Pitt, Earl of Chatham, 1770," in *In Pursuit of Refinement: Charlestonians Abroad, 1740–1860*, ed. Maurie D. McInnis and Angela D. Mack (Columbia: University of South Carolina Press, 1999): 219–21; *South Carolina Gazette*, 9 June 1766, p. 3, col. 1; see also Henry Laurens to John Lewis Gervais, 12 May 1766, *The Papers of Henry Laurens, 1765–1768*, ed. George C. Rogers, Jr. and David R. Chesnutt (Columbia: University of South Carolina Press, 1976), 5:128–29.

89. See Joseph W. Barnwell, ed., "Correspondence of Charles Garth," *South Carolina Historical Magazine* 28 (1927): 79–93.

90. Peter and John Horlbeck, builders of the privies and jailer's house behind the state-house, received the commission to build the base and pedestal of the statue. From 7 June to 7 July 1770, several of the Horlbecks' "prime hands" assisted the English stonemason William Adron in erecting the statue at the intersection of Meeting and Broad Streets. Horlbeck Papers, private collection, Charleston.

91. Quoted in D. E. Huger Smith, "Wilton's Statue of Pitt," *South Carolina Historical Magazine* 15 (1914): 26.

92. For a discussion of the Wilkes Fund Controversy, see Jack P. Greene, ed., *The Nature of Colony Constitutions: Two Pamphlets on the Wilkes Fund Controversy in South Carolina by Sir Egerton Leigh and Arthur Lee* (Columbia: University of South Carolina Press, 1970).

93. Robert Walsh, *Charleston's Sons of Liberty: A Study of the Artisans, 1763–1789* (Columbia: University of South Carolina Press, 1959), 69, 73–74.

94. John Drayton, *Memoirs of the American Revolution as Relating to the State of South Carolina* (1821; reprint, New York: New York Times Books, 1969), 1:167, 222–24.

95. After the war the Pitt statue suffered further indignities. In 1791 it was hit by four vehicles over the course of a few months and was beginning to be considered more a public nuisance in its exposed position than a symbol of a political ideal. The statue was moved from the intersection in 1794 and stored at the Orphan House, where it eventually was re-erected in front of the building. Poston, "Statue of William Pitt," 219

96. Richard Walsh, ed., *The Writings of Christopher Gadsden, 1746–1805* (Columbia: University of South Carolina Press, 1966), 200–201.

97. South Carolina Treasury, Charleston, *Journal, 1783–1791*, South Carolina Department of Archives and History, 12, 18, 43, 55, 67, 82, 83, August 1783, October 1783, July

100   1784, November 1784, February 1785, May 1785. On the function of the privy council, see Adele Stanton Edwards, ed., *Journals of the Privy Council, 1783–1789* (Columbia: University of South Carolina Press, 1971).

98. Frederick Dalcho, *An Historical Account of the Protestant Episcopal Church in South-Carolina* (Charleston: E. Thayer, 1820), 465.

99. The removal of the twentieth-century additions in 1993 revealed the lower section of a late-eighteenth- or early-nineteenth-century lightning conductor still in situ on the north side of the courthouse, just east of the vaulted platform.

100. South Carolina Treasury, *Journal, 1783–1791*, 176, 178, 187, 193, 264, May 1786, June 1786, July 1786, April 1787.

101. *Columbian Herald*, 7 February 1788, p. 2, col. 2.

102. "Autobiography of Benjamin Franklin Perry" (manuscript in the South Caroliniana Library, Columbia), 10.

103. In the 1850s the name of William Drayton, a judge and the head of the rebuilding committee, was mentioned by artist Charles Fraser as the architect of the new work. Drayton's role in the design process was a short-lived one. The judge died in 1790, barely two years after the fire and long before the building was ready for occupancy. Fraser, *Reminiscences of Charleston*, 99–100.

104. The similarities of overall vocabulary and certain elements of the White House and the Charleston County Courthouse have led to an assertion that the Irish immigrant James Hoban may have been responsible for the design of the reconfigured Charleston courthouse. Although he was working in the carpentry business and teaching drafting in Charleston at the time of the fire, no evidence links Hoban with the project. See William Seale, *The President's House*, (Washington, D.C.: White House Historical Associates, 1986), 1:40, 46.

105. Gene Waddell called attention to the similarities of the courthouse facade and several plates illustrated in Gibbs's *Book of Architecture*, first published in 1728. Plate 54, "The Plan and Front of a Design Made for a Person of Quality in 1720," is a three-story nine-bay structure with an engaged, pedimented portico spanning the height of the second and third floors. As in the Charleston courthouse, the second and eighth bays of the second and third floors contain niches. Plate 42, "Plan and Upright of a House 100 Feet in Front and 70 Feet Deep," is of a similar design, without the niches and the engaged columns of the central pedimented three-bay projection. However, this section stands on a rusticated arcade similar to the one devised for the courthouse. Gene Waddell to Margaretta Childs, 9 April 1990 (Historic Charleston Foundation).

106. Although the third-floor windows correspond in width and location to those of the lower two floors, they bear no evidence of alteration. This evidence suggests that the lower openings were shifted when the upper floor was added after the 1788 fire.

107. Owing, however, to an extensive rebuilding of the west facade following the earthquake of 1886, it is impossible to fully verify this hypothesis.

108. The pit-sawn wood of the boxed jambs is mortised into the sill and head. The original sash weights and pulleys were replaced in later alterations. Steven Bauer, "Report on the Demolition of the Charleston County Courthouse" (report for Historic Charleston Foundation, July 1993).

109. The origins of Robert Given are unknown. He appeared in Charleston by the mid-1780s, where he advertised his services as a stonecutter and bricklayer. In 1786 he married Mary Pattison. A few years later they purchased property in Ansonborough and lived on Federal Street. Despite Moultrie's recommendation, there is no indication that Given worked in

Washington on the federal buildings in the early 1790s. However, in 1795 Given was hired to work in Philadelphia on the First Bank of the United States, a two-story building with a stone facade and pedimented Corinthian portico designed by Samuel Blodgett, Jr. After the completion of that project, Given was back in Charleston plying his trade as a stonecutter and carver. In the fall of 1797 he purchased a cargo of Virginia freestone, which, he advertised, was fit for windowsills, arches, and steps for doors. He also noted his ability to cut and carve chimneypieces and gravestones. Given died in Charleston in 1801 or 1802. I am grateful to Christine Patrick, editor of the Papers of George Washington, for bringing the reference to the federal buildings to my attention. William Moultrie to George Washington, 24 August 1792, National Archives, Washington, D.C., Record Group 42, General Records, Letters Received, 1791–1867. For other aspects of Given's career, see *Charleston Morning Post and Daily Advertiser,* 21 November 1786, p. 2, col. 2; *The City Gazette, or The Daily Advertiser,* 17 September 1788, p. 2, col. 2; Charleston County *Land Records Miscellaneous,* Part 83, Books K6–L6, 1793–1794, 16 January 1792, 360–61; *The City Gazette and the Daily Advertiser,* 13 April 1795, p. 3, col. 2; 28 November 1797, p. 4, col. 1; *Negrin's Directory and Almanac for the Year 1802* (Charleston: J. J. Negrin's Press, 1802).

110. On the brickwork of the inside walls, the absence of arched heads and a single tier of closers on these niches contrasts with all other original openings, affirming that windows preceded construction of niches on the lower two floors.

111. General Assembly Papers 0010 003 1828 00039 00, 18 November 1828; 0010 003 1828 00038 00, 1828.

112. *Charleston Courier,* 16 September 1835.

113. See, for example, a resolution passed by the General Assembly a week after the fire. General Assembly Papers, 0010 016 1788 00002 00, 11 February 1788, Columbia, South Carolina Department of Archives and History.

114. Maeva Marcus, ed., *The Documentary History of the Supreme Court of the United States, 1789–1800,* vol. 2., *The Justices on Circuit, 1790–1794* (New York: Columbia University Press, 1988), 322–24.

115. General Assembly Papers 0010 015 1796 00001 00, September 1796.

116. Diary of Edward Hooker, 31 October 1805 (original manuscript in the Connecticut Historical Society, Hartford, Conn.).

117. General Assembly Papers 0010 003 1809 00053 00, 5 December 1808. Bricklayer Anthony Toomer had worked on many projects throughout the city since the 1760s. In 1767 he received the contract to build a bridge over a creek on East Bay Street near the present corner of Market Street. During the period he was repairing and rebuilding the walls of the courthouse, he received several major commissions. In 1792 he was hired to construct the brick walls of the three-story orphans' house, a building far larger than the courthouse. In the same year, he was contracted to undertake the brickwork of a new theater on Savage's Green, a structure that may have been designed by the Irish carpenter James Hoban, who had resided briefly in Charleston. Ravenel, *Architects of Charleston,* 42, 78, 81.

118. *The (Charleston) Times,* 5 September 1808, p. 3, col. 3.

119. The discovery of split lath secured by hand-headed cut nails in the ceiling near the stair testifies to this belated work.

120. General Assembly Papers 0010 003 1809 00060 00, 30 August 1809.

121. Scarcely had the interior been finished when more than $1,400 in major repairs were undertaken in 1818. This work included carpentry, glazing, painting, and brickwork. "Report of the Civil and Military Engineer of the State of South Carolina, for the Year

102   1816," *Internal Improvement in South Carolina, 1817–1828,* ed. David Kohn (Washington, D.C., n.p., 1938), 1.

122. Robert Mills, *Statistics of South Carolina* (Charleston: Hurlbut and Lloyd, 1826), 408.

123. Caroline Gilman, "Descriptive Sketch of a Part of Meeting-Street in Charleston," *The Southern Rose* 7 (September 1838): 1–2, quoted in Kenneth Severens, *Charleston: Antebellum Architecture and Civic Destiny* (Knoxville: University of Tennessee Press, 1988), 114.

124. The Courts of Common Pleas and General Sessions had "original jurisdiction in all civil cases where *legal* rights are involved (except in matters of contract, where the amount is $20 or under) and in all criminal cases, affecting free white men; and appellate jurisdiction, in all appeals from Magistrates' Courts, and in appeals from the Court of Ordinary; in all cases except in matters of account. The times for holding the court for Charleston District, are the first Monday in May, to sit six weeks, and the fourth Monday in October, to sit four weeks." *The Charleston City and General Business Directory for 1855* (Charleston: David Gazlay, 1855), 1:47. The locations of the offices and courts during the early nineteenth century can be traced through the various city directories that survive for this period. See, for example, Abraham Motte, comp., *Charleston Directory and Stranger's Guide, for the Year 1816* (Charleston, 1816).

125. In a plea to enlarge the bar in a number of southern Virginia county courts, one member of the legal profession lamented his colleagues' condition:

> "Confin'd within a compass three yards long,
> We scarce can stand amidst the brawling throng,
> Wedg'd in by shoulders, outstretch'd arms and knees,
> Each poor Attorney scarce can fairly squeeze
> His carcase to a seat within the bar,
> Or stir his joints, so crouded is he there."

William Munford, *Poems and Compositions in Prose on Several Occasions* (Richmond: Samuel Pleasant, 1798), 146. For the absence of decorum in a Vermont courtroom, see Edward Rendall, *Travels through the Northern Part of the United States* (New York, 1809), 249.

126. *Negrin's Directory and Almanac for the Year 1806* (Charleston: J. J. Negrin's Press, 1806).

127. Samples of early plaster were examined by historic paint color consultant Frank Welsh. Results of his laboratory analysis are contained in a report to Jonathan Poston of Historic Charleston Foundation, 10 August 1991.

128. The Courts of Equity encompassed "all matters belonging to a Court of Equity, as contradistinguished from a court of law." In Charleston the court term was held "on the first Monday in February, to sit six weeks, and on the second Monday in June, to sit four weeks." *The Charleston City and General Business Directory for 1855,* 1:47. When the federal court was not in session, local societies made use of the room from time to time. In 1813 the Literary and Philosophical Society held one of its organizational meetings in the courtroom. *(Charleston) City Gazette and Commercial Advertiser,* 10 August 1813, p. 3, col. 2.

129. Marcus, *The Justices on the Circuit Court, 1790–1794,* 322–24; William and Jane Pease, *James Louis Petigru: Southern Conservative, Southern Dissenter* (Athens: University of Georgia Press, 1995), 45; and Alexander Moore, "Charleston County Federal District Court House Sites" (manuscript on file in U.S. District Court, Strom Thurmond Building, Columbia, S.C., 1997), 6–7.

130. Marcus, *The Justices on Circuit Court, 1790–1794.* See also U.S. Circuit Court Book, 1790–1809, bk. 1, no. 392, National Archives, East Point, Georgia.

131. Eleanor Schwartz, "Hard Traveling Justices," *Constitution* (Winter 1990): 23.

132. U.S. Circuit Court Minute Book, 1790–1809, no. 1, 25 October 1795, 76, National Archives, East Point, Georgia.

133. "Diary of a Journey through the U. S.," 25 May 1823 (manuscript, New-York Historical Society), 1272–74.

134. Welsh to Poston, 10 August 1991.

135. Albert Simons and Samuel Lapham, eds., *The Early Architecture of Charleston* (1927; reprint, Columbia: University of South Carolina Press, 1970), 164–67.

136. Mills, *Statistics of South Carolina,* 408.

137. General Assembly Papers 0010 004 1826 00221 00, 1826; O. Cromwell, comp., *Directory of the City of Charleston, for 1829* (Charleston: James S. Burges, 1828), 6.

138. Charles Parker Agenda Journal, 1857, S. Lewis Simons Collection, South Carolina Historical Society. The Courts for the Correction of Errors consisted "of all the judges in law and equity [convened], to try constitutional questions, or questions where the law and equity courts are divided, and which are referred thereto by either of the courts, are held at such times, and during the sitting of the Court of Appeals, as the chancellors and judges may appoint." *The Charleston City and General Business Directory for 1855,* 1:47.

139. Mills, *Statistics of South Carolina,* 408.

140. Minutes of the Medical Society of South Carolina, 1789–1810, Waring Library, Medical University of South Carolina, 138, 140; Minutes of the Medical Society, 1810–1825, 40.

141. Severens, *Charleston: Antebellum Architecture and Civic Destiny,* 48–50.

142. Richard Beale Davis, *Intellectual Life in the Colonial South, 1587–1763* (Knoxville: University of Tennessee Press, 1978), 2:522–24.

143. *The Charleston Courier,* 24 October 1807.

144. *Bulletin of the Charleston Museum* (October 1906), 2:48–54.

145. *The Charleston Courier,* 4 September 1807.

146. Hooker diary, 56.

147. John Lambert, *Travels through Lower Canada and the United States of North America in the Years 1806, 1807, and 1808* (London: Richard Phillips, 1810), 2:363–65. For other descriptions, see also Duke de la Rochefoucauld Liancourt, *Travels through the United States of North America, the Country of the Iroquois, and Upper Canada in the Years 1795, 1796, and 1798* (London: R. Phillips, 1799), 2:425; Sidney Martin, ed., "Ebenezer Kellogg's Visit to Charleston, 1817," *South Carolina Historical and Genealogical Magazine* 49 (1948): 12; and Lucius Moffatt, ed., "A Frenchman Visits Charleston, 1817," *South Carolina Historical and Genealogical Magazine* 49 (1948): 147.

148. Martin, "Ebenezer Kellogg's Visit to Charleston, 1817," 12.

149. "1810–Diary of J. P. Dunlop, Charleston"(manuscript, New-York Historical Society).

150. *Directory of the City of Charleston, for 1829,* 6.

151. James Smith, comp., *The Charleston Directory; and Register for 1835–1836* (Charleston: Daniel J. Dowling, 1835), 143.

152. For a comparison, see Gene Waddell and Rhodri Windsor Liscombe, *Robert Mills's Courthouses and Jails* (Easley, S.C.: Southern Historical Press, 1981).

153. General Assembly Papers 0010 015 1854 00005 00, Fall 1854.

154. General Assembly Papers 0010 015 1856 00007 00, and 0010 015 1856 00008 00, Fall 1856.

155. In 1859 the grand jury noted the small improvements that had been made by painting, whitewashing, and carpeting the interior of the courthouse but felt that "they have just cause

104   to complain that the improvements did not extend to the room of the Grand Jury. It is neither comfortable nor healthy to sit for hours in a cold, uncarpeted room, that has been closed for months." General Assembly Papers 0010 015 1859 00016 00, January 1859.

156. *Charleston Mercury,* 20 October 1860.

157. Waddell and Liscombe, *Robert Mills's Courthouses and Jails.*

158. *Charleston Mercury,* 20 October 1860.

159. *Charleston Daily Courier,* 8 January 1866, p. 2, col. 2; 9 January 1866, p. 2, col. 2.

160. *Charleston News and Courier,* 29 June 1883, p. 4, col. 1.

161. Mazyck noted that "the first floor comprises a large central hall and the rooms of the officers of the court. From the hall a broad staircase leads to the second floor, the western portion of which is the present court-room; the eastern, formerly the Equity Court-room, is now used as the clerk's office and depository of the books of the court. The third floor contains the jury-rooms." Arthur Mazyck, *Charleston South Carolina in 1883* (Boston: Heliotype Printing Company, 1883), 2–3.

162. *Charleston News and Courier,* 26 July 1883, p. 1, col. 8.

163. Quoted in Milner Associates, "Charleston County Courthouse: A Historic Structure Report," 21.

164. *The Charleston News and Courier,* 26 July 1883, p. 1, col. 8.

165. Ibid., 16 February 1884, p. 1, col. 5.

166. Ibid.

167. Ibid.

168. Ibid., 19 February 1884, p. 1, col. 6.

169. Ibid.

170. Ibid.

171. Arthur Mazyck, *Charleston in 1885* (Charleston: Walker, Evans, Cogswell, 1885), 11–12; *Charleston News and Courier,* 23 June 1883, p. 1, col. 8.

172. The report recommended that "cracks over openings" should be "well repaired and plastering throughout. North and south walls anchored at each story." H. A. Stockdell et al., "Record of Earthquake Damages" (Atlanta, 1886), 50–221, manuscript in the South Carolina Historical Society.

173. *Charleston News and Courier,* 21 and 22 March 1926.

174. Ibid., 13 and 26 May 1926.

175. Ibid., 6 July 1926.

176. Ibid.

177. Ibid., 29 August 1926.

178. Ibid., 7 and 12 January 1927.

179. Ibid., 25 November 1940.

180. *The Charleston Evening Post,* 13 December 1940.

181. *Charleston News and Courier,* 25 November 1940.

182. Ibid.

183. *The Charleston Evening Post,* 7 and 29 November 1949; 8 and 9 December 1949.

184. *Charleston News and Courier,* 4 April 1966.

185. Milner Associates, "Charleston County Courthouse: A Historic Structure Report," 52.

186. *Charleston News and Courier,* 5 January 1969.

187. For the role of Historic Charleston Foundation in the courthouse project, see Robert R. Weyeneth, *Historic Preservation for a Living City: Historic Charleston Foundation, 1947–1997*

(Columbia: University of South Carolina Press, 1999), 186–90. For the earlier study of the   105
courthouse, see Milner Associates, "Charleston County Courthouse: A Historic Structure
Report." For the work of the consultants to Historic Charleston Foundation, see Carl Lounsbury, Willie Graham, Mark R. Wenger, and W. Brown Morton III, "An Architectural Analysis
of the Charleston County Courthouse" and "The Future of the Charleston County Courthouse: Recommendations to the Charleston County Council," August 1991. See also *The
(Charleston) News and Courier,* 16 and 18 August 1991.

188. *Charleston News and Courier,* 20 and 22 September 1991.

INDEX